BUILDING
a blended
FAMILY

A Guide to Strengthening
Stepfamily Relationships,

The True Story of
One Family's Challenge

PHIL COLLINS

TATE PUBLISHING, LLC

DEDICATION

Without the strength and direction of God the Father, Building a Blended Family would have never been written. First and foremost it is through my personal relationship with Jesus Christ that our family has survived and this book is made possible. To Him be all the glory and praise.

Building a Blended Family is also dedicated to my wife Marie whose love, support and perseverance contributed greatly to the publication of this book. Special thanks to my friends Larry and Dianne Wilbanks. Their gift of love and obedience also made the publication of this book possible.

Introduction to Building a Blended Family

What you are about to read is the real life story of a family (my family) facing the trials, tribulations and victories of building a blended family. This book serves as a guideline explaining the dos and don'ts on how to effectively build a blended family. Building a Blended Family is compelling, transparent and from the heart like no other book on blended families.

Although the challenges are great, with Jesus Christ as the nucleus of our home, we will survive. The foundation for blended families in America today must be built upon Biblical principles found in God's Word and the teachings of Jesus Christ.

Building a strong family blended is a process, it requires, love, forgiveness, understanding, patience, and commitment. It takes time and doesn't happen overnight, however through Christ, the study of God's Word, strong family units and values can be built on solid foundations designed to weather any storm.

There are many struggles that face the blended family today. I have experienced many of those trials, tribulations and struggles, as I've attempted to build a blended family. I have also seen many victories resulting through faith in Jesus Christ.

It is my prayer that as you read this book, you will open your heart to God; allow Him to work in your life, marriage and the life of your blended family. My greatest prayer is that if you do not know Jesus Christ in a personal way, you will find Him as you read and study Building a Blended Family. He is waiting for you. Just ask Him into your heart and life. **The greatest gift you and your blended family will ever receive is free. . . . the gift of eternal life through faith in Jesus Christ**.

May God Bless You,
Phil Collins

My Story

I grew up in a traditional family where I was the only child. I was raised in church, taken every Sunday rain, or shine, and although I didn't want to go at times, I am very thankful I had parents who strongly encouraged me to go (if you know what I mean). Growing up in the 60s, it was rare to hear of divorce between a husband and wife. I do not remember having friends whose parents had "split up" much less divorced. The word "stepchild," or "stepchildren" was seldom mentioned or used in one's daily vocabulary, unlike today.

I do not remember the *"D"* word being mentioned until I was in my teen years. Divorce was a word associated with individuals who were perceived as being different and failures. Little did I know that one day I would be looked upon as a second class citizen and failure by those closest to me?

I have learned very quickly that discrimination comes in many forms and from many different arenas, often shunned by the very people who profess to love and forgive you. I can remember individuals being looked upon as failures because their marriages ended in divorce. As you will soon read in the following paragraphs that is to the contrary. Let us begin.

As I stated earlier, divorce was a word never mentioned and something that should never have happened to me when I married. I was married in 1979 and fully expected to remain married until parted by death. It is amazing how things change so quickly. In the early days of my marriage, I fully expected to have the fairytale union everyone dreamed of—the home, the perfect career, the perfect family, and money. As the years passed, the family I dreamed of began to fall apart. My career became more important and money was my life

Without going into detail, my marriage ended 13 years after it began. Let me say that I was given three beautiful children as a result of that marriage. Many emotions were birthed after my divorce, but none would compare to the feelings of failure and guilt over missing my children.

Many blended families have been started by husbands, wives, fathers, step mothers, mothers and step fathers who bring feelings of guilt, unforgiveness, anger and failure into the relationship at its very beginning. It is so important to assess and deal with *any and all* emotional baggage before starting a relationship that could lead to marriage and the creation of a blended family.

After my divorce I entered into the dating scene immediately. I made many mistakes, dated when I should not have, and failed to seek God for direction when I should have. Yet, God was in control and protecting me.

August 20th, 1995 11:00 A.M.

At a small church in a small town in North Carolina during the 11 o'clock Sunday morning service, I made my way down to the altar and made a decision that would change my life forever. I asked Jesus Christ into my life. Prior to that experience, I thought that I was a Christian, but all along I was only playing the game like so many do.

That day and prior to it, I had been struggling with many issues in my life, but on that faithful Sunday morning, I came to find real peace and joy.

Although I missed my children so much, I was able to face the pain knowing I had a friend closer than a brother to help me. Even now at times my heart stills aches because I cannot hold my children close. Two of my children live over 1000 miles away, and although I miss them dearly, I am comforted by God's love and mercy, knowing the He will take care of them.

June 1998

In June 1998, I began to pray for God's direction in my life and if it be His will to send someone into my life. Prayer must become a part of everyday blended family life. On Father's Day that June, I went to church as always, never intending to meet anyone. A friend of mine told me of a woman who was single with children.

That Sunday morning he pointed her out to me. I remember looking up and seeing this beautiful blonde lady in the balcony.

Then as I looked to her left, I noticed she had children. I later found out that this beautiful lady had four boys. I had convinced myself that I would not marry anyone who had children. Well, as the old saying goes, "never say never." The following Wednesday night I met Marie. It was the Wednesday night church service. After the service we stood on the steps outside the church she attended and talked. We talked for almost two hours to be exact. Her youngest son stood still listening to every word without becoming bored—a true miracle.

Our initial conversation was not the typical one to which I had become accustomed. The first words that proceeded out of Marie's mouth were, "Do you know Jesus Christ as your Lord and Savior?" WOW! What a question. We had one awesome spiritual conversation. The next week my oldest daughter met Marie and fell in love with her. We had lunch with Marie and three of her sons. They too accepted me with open arms, especially Josh who appeared to really want us together.

Without going into all the details, we began to date. One of the first things we promised God and each other was that if we entered into a serious relationship, we would keep it Christ centered without allowing sexual urges, or desires to overcome us and destroy what God had placed together. I cannot over emphasize the importance of keeping a premarital relationship sex free. Never enter into a blended family relationship with physical desires and attractions at the fore front.

We fulfilled our commitment, and it was worth it all. We began dating and on November 14, 1998, we were married. After our honeymoon we thought all would be well, not knowing that in just three weeks we would face one of the most unreal and unexpected battles in our lives, which you will read about later in the book.

Marriage in a blended family must be carefully planned. Strategies must be developed in an attempt to prepare the biological and step parent for the unexpected. Of course we all know that just when we think we've adequately prepared for the unexpected, the unexpected will occur.

Careful planning must be considered especially when children are involved. Statistics indicate that during the next 5 years, about half of all families with children will be in a blended family.

Years ago, most families were a close-knit unit, spending time together, sharing meals with one another and communicating. Today's families are headed towards the opposite end of the spectrum, moving away from the blueprints God designed for the family.

TABLE OF CONTENTS

CHAPTER 1

What Happened to the Traditional American Family?

What happened to the American family as we once knew it? Consider the American family today, in relationship to the American family of yesteryear. America and the Christian faith, was built upon the foundation of God's Word, His principles, the teachings of Christ, His life and the family. The family as we once knew it, the Ozzie and Harriett if you will, rarely exist. Years ago, marriage was the central institution under which households were organized and children raised.

The U.S Census Bureau has reported that blended families are one of the largest family groups in our country today, headed towards becoming the largest family group in our country. Other more recent surveys suggest that blended families are in fact the predominant family unit in America today. Recent studies revealed that 50% of children living in America under the age of 13 live in a blended family setting.

In America the family as we once knew it, is all but a thing of the past. Families are being destroyed by the temptations of this world and our society. Divorce is rampant and children, the innocent victims, are affected drastically. What can we do to stop the problems facing families today? What can we do to stop the problems and issues corrupting families today? What can you do to make a positive impact on your family? Will you "go against the grain" to make a difference?

In America there are several types of family settings far different from the traditional family as we once knew it. Here are a few examples:

1. Single parent homes due to divorce, death, abandonment
2. Mothers never married with children
3. Fathers never married with children
4. Step Families
5. Blended Families
6. Foster Families

STATISTICS:

In our American society, only 30% of families admit to sitting down at the dinner table once, or twice a week and sharing a meal. In a recent survey of 5,000 teenagers from different sections of America, 15% said they felt they could talk to their parents, 41% said their parents didn't care and 44% said they preferred TV and video games as opposed to spending time with their parents.

Does this explain the reason why our country is in such disarray? What happened? The answer to the question is very simple. We've drifted away from the very thing this great nation of ours was founded upon—belief in God, His Word, and the instruction given to us by the life of Christ. Before we continue, take a few moments and review the following information.

Below is an overview of the standard of living for the average family in the 1950's.

FAMILY LIFE AND CULTURE IN THE FIFTIES:

Take a few minutes to review and consider the following information regarding the family of the 1950's as opposed to the family of today.

Did you know that in the 1950's, almost 1/3 of all 19 yr. old females were married.

The divorce rate was **1 in every 10 marriages**; divorce **was unacceptable** then.

Families bonded and connected by doing various activities together such as:

Attending church
Going on trips and vacationing together at least once a year
Attending family reunions
Going to sporting events together
Watching TV
Working in the yard
Washing cars together

In 1957 the birthrate peaked with 4.3 million new babies being born. Very few women had a desire to work. Only 19.3% of women were working in 1951. About 1/2 (47%) of college students were females in 1920, as opposed to 35% in 1950. Is it safe to assume by the statistics that women felt raising a family and family life in general was more important.

CURRENT FAMILY STATISTICS AND CHILDREN

Between 1970 and the present, the proportion of children under 18 years of age living with one parent has grown from 12 percent to 28 percent. 68.7% of American Youth are living in non-traditional families 7 out of 10.

Other studies and statistics indicate that. . . .

26.3% are living with biological mother (Stepfamily Association)
5.4% are living with biological father (Stepfamily Association)
1% are living in Foster Families (U.S. Census Bureau)
3.7% are living with non-relatives (U.S. Census Bureau)
6.3% are living with grandparents (AARP - U.S. Census Bureau)
30% are living in blended families. (Stepfamily Association)

1.2% live with non relatives outside foster care

The divorce rate still stands at around 50% for first time marriages with an average of around 60% for second and third marriages. With divorce made easier due to no fault divorces, an increase in separation and divorce is very likely. These current trends and rates of divorce affect the overall picture of the family and the emotional well being of children in America and across the world today.

DIVORCE AND RE-MARRIAGE STATISTICAL OVERVIEW:

The divorce rate in the United States is the highest in the world.

Approximately 50% of first time marriages will eventually end in a documented legal divorce.

Approximately 60% of all remarriages will end in a documented legal divorce.

Approximately 75% of all divorced individuals at some point remarry.

Approximately 45% of all marriages in America are remarriages for at least one of the new spouses.

Approximately 65% of remarriages will include, or will involve children from a prior marriage, thereby forming a blended family.

Less than 50% of children who are directly related to a divorce, do well after a parent / parents separate or divorce.

Considering the following. . . . .

1. 1 in 2 children will live in a single parent family at some point in childhood
2. 1 in 3 children is born to unmarried parents
3. 1 in 4 children lives with only one parent
4. 1 in 8 children is born to a teenage mother
5. 1 in 25 children lives with neither parent

(The State of America's Children, 1998 Year-book, Children's Defense Fund)

Children of divorced parents are seven times more likely to suffer from depression in adult life than people of similar age and background whose parents have not divorced. This Israeli study indicated that the loss of a parent through divorce is more likely to cause depression than loss through death. "The earlier the separation occurred, the more likely it was to have had an influence," researcher Bernard Lerer said. *(Study by Bernard Lerer and Ofer Agid of the Biological Psychiatric Unit at Hadassah Hospital, Jerusalem, as reported in Molecular Psychiatry, 1999)*

STEPFAMILY STATISTICS

It is estimated that 1,300 new blended families are being formed everyday. With the increase in blended family formations, all the more reason to address the needs and concerns associated with blended family life.

Consider that . . . .

1 of every 3 Americans is now a stepparent, stepchild, or in some manner associated with a blended family.

More than 50% of all Americans today were involved in the past, currently involved, or at some point in the future will be involved in a blended family relationship.

At the present children reside in a stepfather, or stepfather/ stepmother combination blended family. In most cases a stepfather's biological children do not reside with him in the blended family setting.

Current trends and studies suggest that if the blended family is not already the largest family group in America today that by the year 2010 it will be.

These statistics necessitate the need for working hard at making any and all newly developed blended families successful.

CUSTODIAL / NON-CUSTODIAL STATISTICS

Fathers without visitation or joint custody pay only 44.5% of child support owed, but fathers with visitation pay 79.1% of child support owed.

Fathers with joint custody pay 90.2% of child support owed.

The number of single-parent homes has skyrocketed, displacing many children in this country. Approximately 30% of U.S. families are now being headed by a single parent, and in 80% of those families, the mother is the sole parent. The United States is the world's leader in fatherless families.

Father absence contributes to crime and delinquency. Violent criminals are overwhelmingly males who grew up without fathers. *(U.S. Census Bureau report, "Child Support and Alimony: 1989, released Oct. 11, 1991)*

BEHAVIOR STATISTICS

75% of children/adolescents in chemical dependency hospitals are from single-parent families. *(Center for Disease Control, Atlanta, GA)*

1 out of 5 children have a learning, emotional, or behavioral problem due to a change in their family structure. *(National Center for Health Statistics)*

More than one half of all youths incarcerated for criminal acts lived in one-parent families when they were children. *(Children's Defense Fund)*

Nine million American children face risk factors that may hinder their ability to become healthy and productive adults. One in seven children deal with at least four of the risk factors, which include growing up in a single-parent household . . . The survey also indicated that children confronting several risk factors are more likely to experience problems with concentration, communication, and health. *(1999 Kids Count Survey - Annie E. Casey Foundation)*

SUICIDE STATISTICS

Every 78 seconds a teen attempts suicide - every 90 seconds they succeed. *(National Center for Health Statistics)*

63% of suicides are individuals from single parent families *(FBI Law Enforcement Bulletin - Investigative Aid)*

"Separation, divorce and unmarried parenthood seemed to be a high risk for children/adolescents in these families for the development of suicidal behavior." *(Atilla Turgay, M.D. American Psychiatric Association's Scientific Meeting, May 1994)*

TEEN PREGNANCY STATISTICS

75% of teenage pregnancies are adolescents from single parent homes *(Children in need: Investment Strategies . . . Committee for Economic Development)*

Approximately 13% of all babies born in the U.S. are born to adolescent mothers, with one million teens becoming pregnant each year. Explanations for teen pregnancy include the break-up of the American home and parental loss. *(University of Kentucky, Departments of Psychiatry, Ob/Gyn and Psychology)*

Today's departures from the traditional family are on the rise. Take into consideration the following:

Persons living alone account for approximately 25% of American households

One out of every 5 children is born is to an unwed mother, 3 out of every 5 children born this year will live in a single-parent household for at least part of their childhood.

1 out 3 children treated for mental disorders this year will be teenagers,

1 out of 10 young boys has been sexually assaulted in their own home,

1 out of 3 women has been sexually assaulted before

they were 18 with 80% of the assaults occurring in their own home, making it the most dangerous place for young women.

In 1998, a survey of 10,000 American households was conducted by the University of Ohio, to determine how separation, divorce, substance abuse, physical abuse, teen problems, etc. affect home life in America today. The study revealed that 94% of the households surveyed are somewhat dysfunctional as a result of separation, divorce, remarriage and family issues affecting the family unit.

With the rapid changing trend in the American family system today, it has been reported that the U.S. Census Bureau has decided to discontinue providing estimates of marriage, divorce, and remarriage except for those that are available from previously recorded census. What does this tell us about the American family? Does this support the fact that 64% of families today in our country live in some type of divorced, and or blended family / step family relationship?

Current statistics underestimate the number of U.S. stepfamilies, because . . .

The family as we once new it, is changing at such a drastic rate, it is difficult to keep track with all the new data. So if the child lives with a divorced parent, single parent and the other nonresident parent has remarried, the child is not included in the calculations as being a member of a blended family.

Estimation efforts by Bumpass, Raley, and Sweet (1995), using data from 1987–1988 suggest that many children living in a "single parent household" (as designated by the Census Bureau) are actually living with two adults. Thus, their best estimates indicate that about 25% of current stepfamilies are actually cohabiting couples.

They show that if only children residing in legally married stepfamilies are included, 23% of children would be designated as living in a stepfamily.

When children are included who live with a cohabiting parent, the figure rises to 30%, they suggest that 66% of all women, and 30% of all children, are likely to spend some time in a stepfamily, using the more liberal definition that includes cohabiting adult couples.

SOURCES:

Bumpass, L.L., Raley, R.K., & Sweet, J.A. (1995). "The changing character of stepfamilies: Implications of cohabitation and nonmarital childbearing," *Demography* 32, 425–436.

Glick, P.C. (1989), "Remarried families, stepfamilies, and stepchildren: A brief demographic profile," *Family Relations* 38, 24- 28.

Glick, P.C. & Lin, S.L. (1987), "Remarriage after divorce: Recent changes and demographic variation," *Sociological Perspectives* 30(2), 162- 167.

Larson, J. (1992), "Understanding stepfamilies," *American Demographics* 14, 360.

Norton, A.J., & Miller, L.F. (1992), "Marriage, Divorce, and Remarriage in the 1990s," *Current Population Reports* (Series P23–180), Washington, DC: Government Printing Office

U.S. Bureau of the Census (1998), "Marital Satus and Living Arrangements," *Current Population Reports* (Series P20–514), Washington, DC: Government Printing Office.

Although the information appears to be outdated, statistics suggest and supports the fact that blended families are on the rise and shall remain so indefinitely. What do think a blended family is composed of? After reading these statistics, is it easier to understand why the family is being challenged and blended families are on the rise?

CONSIDER THE FOLLOWING QUESTIONS CAREFULLY.

1. In your opinion, what do you think happened to the family, as we know it today?

_____
_____
_____
_____
_____

2. Can you think of ways to return the family back to the way it was in the 50s and 60s? Or can we?

_____
_____
_____
_____
_____

3. What would our society be like?

_____
_____
_____
_____
_____

4. How do we prevent and or reduce the problems faced by blended families today?

_____
_____
_____
_____
_____

5. What should we do to change the stigma currently attached to the family?

_____

_____

_____

_____

_____

CHAPTER 2

God's Plan for the Blended Family

A Blended family consists of a man and woman married with children from a previous marriage(s) and one or both of the adults are raising a child or children who are not biologically theirs.

What do we mean by original families, traditional, or nuclear families? Original families consist of a man and woman married, with children, both being the biological parents who have never divorced.

God ordained the family as the foundational institution of human society. The mind set is that the family is composed of persons related to one another by marriage, blood, etc. While that may be true, so many families are now intertwined with non-biological members. Two things form the foundation of America; our belief in God almighty and the family. Can a blended family be part of our country's foundation as well? Will God bless a blended family? Yes! These questions and others will be answered in later chapters.

Marriage is the uniting of one man and one woman in covenant commitment for the rest of their lives, thereby creating the earthly foundation for the family. It is God's unique gift to reveal the union between Christ and His church and to provide for the man and the woman in marriage the framework for intimate companionship, which is the channel for sexual expression according to biblical standards, and the means of developing a

Christ centered family unit. The same applies for married couples in a blended family environment. In my opinion there are no exceptions, and the martial commitment should be treated the same in a blended family as it would be in a traditional family.

The husband and wife are of equal worth before God since both are created in God's image. The marriage relationship is designed as a method in which God relates to His people. A husband is to love his wife as Christ loved the church and do what it takes to understand her and her needs. He has the God-given responsibility to provide, protect, and lead his family. This applies to husbands in the blended family as well. Wives need husbands who are men of God without exception.

A wife is to submit herself graciously to the servant leadership of her husband even as the church willingly submits to the leadership of Christ. She, being in the image of God as is her husband and thus equal to him, has the God-given responsibility to respect her husband and to serve as his helper in managing the household and nurturing the next generation. The same applies to wives in a blended family as well. Husbands need wives who are women of God without exception.

Children, from the moment of conception, are a blessing and heritage from the Lord. Parents are to demonstrate to their children God's pattern for marriage. As parents and stepparents, **we are instructed** in God's Word to teach and train our children in the way they should go.

Proverbs 22:6 . . . Train up a child in the way he should go, And even when he is old he will not depart from it.

We are instructed to teach our children and stepchildren the spiritual things of God and commandments as outlined in His Word. It is imperative that as Christian fathers, stepfathers, mothers and stepmothers, we live a consistent lifestyle exemplified by the light of Christ that shines forth from within us.

Parents, love and discipline your child and make choices based on biblical truths.

GOD'S BLUEPRINT FOR THE BLENDED FAMILY:

From the time Adam and Eve walked the earth; God installed and instituted the family. Adam and Eve were created to be on the first page of God's blueprints for the family. Throughout the Bible, you will find how important the family is to God as He plans, constructs and prepares timeless principles for man and the family.

God's construction work is perfect. He used His building skills to bind man and woman together as one to engage in a perfect union for spiritual fulfillment, worship, ministry, companionship, dominion and procreation.

In order to have a strong marriage, a secure family and strength to face the everyday trials of blended family life, we need to read and follow God's Word. For example, let us say we have decided to make the biggest financial investment of our life and build a house. We want to build a house that is sturdy, able to protect us from storms, strong winds, heavy rain, etc, and last for years.

Before we build, we want to make sure our house is built in a neighborhood safe for our family. We look for good schools and conveniences, only the best for our family. Now with that behind us, it's time to locate a builder who is experienced, trustworthy, guarantees his work, and takes pride in what he does. Our builder has a reputation for using the finest materials available to construct a new home, and he builds only on good solid foundations.

The **blueprints** are ready and construction begins. It takes several months; however when the work is finished, a beautiful house, built from raw materials and hard work, stands tall, ready to provide protection for our family. The finished product is a new dwelling place.

God is the main contractor and Jesus Christ the foreman on the job. Jesus gives direction on how to build our spiritual house through the blueprints found in God's Word and the life He (Jesus) lived while on earth. When we accept Jesus Christ as the Lord and Savior of our lives, the old carnal house is demolished and new construction begins.

Using God's Word as our new foundation and construction material, we can build a spiritual dwelling full of life and happiness. In order to guard against the heat of the enemy and repel the heavy rains from the storms of life, we protect our dwelling by using the bricks and paint of God's Word. If we fail to maintain our spiritual house, its value will depreciate rapidly and someday collapse in ruins. God's Word was and still is the blueprint for the family. We must love one another, be thankful for the gift God has given us and protect the house that keeps the family safe.

The home is an illustration to man of God's perfect love for His children. Without godly homes, there would be no church. A blended family built upon the principles of God's Word and a personal relationship with Jesus Christ has the potential of giving society and the world a "word about God" by revealing that there can be life, peace, joy, and happiness after divorce and in blended family life.

By letting society and a world that is indifferent to spiritual truths know there is hope for blended families, we can provide a powerful witness of God's love for all to see.

What a *blueprint* the engineer and designer of this world has placed before us.

1. Are you following God's blueprint for your family? If not, it would be prudent to begin today.
2. Secondly, are there issues in your family that requires change or revision

O YES   O NO

If you checked yes, write your answers in the space provided below.

_____

_____

_____

_____

_____

Could these issues if left unresolved create conflict, or continued conflict?

If there are issues and concerns in your blended family, the next step is to develop a ***Blended Family Action Plan***. Your BFAP should consist of the following 4 components:

- Identifying the problem(s)
- The cause of the problem(s)
- Methods to address and correct the problem(s)
- Goals and objectives to prevent reoccurrence

Before you develop your action plan it would be very beneficial to take inventory of your marriage. Taking the time to complete this process is well worth the effort and may save your marriage / family from unnecessary heartache and strife. You can take it from me; IT WORKS!

TAKING INVENTORY OF YOUR MARRIAGE

Before we continue, take a moment and fill out the following survey as husband and wife. Be honest and answer all the questions **together**. On the following page, answer the questions yes, no, or sometimes.

1. Do I know God through a personal relationship with Jesus Christ?

2. Do I (we) live a life pleasing before God, our family and others?

3. Do we pray together?

4. Do we read the Bible?
(Separately, or together?)

5. Do we pray at mealtime with our family?

6. Do we attend church? **(on a regular basis)**

7. Do I (we) live according to God's Word?

8. Do we treat each other as a husband and wife should according to God's Word?

9. As a couple, are we in complete submission to God?

10. Do others see me (us) differently than who we really are?
(Who knows yourself any better than you and, or your spouse.)

If you answered no, or sometimes to any of the questions in the survey, I challenge you to seek God for direction, add the items that need to be addressed to your BFAP, and make the necessary changes in your life as soon as possible. Doing so will impact your marriage and family for years to come.

CHAPTER 3

Spirit Guided Relationships for the Husband and Wife

In today's society, the blended family is under attack from various forces; forces such as adultery, money, fame, materialism, etc. The husband and wife are major players in the family unit, and as leaders of the home, they need to be aware of the forces that wage war against them, their family, and especially the children.

The husband and wife are under attack as well. We are a unique unit joined together by God, designed by Him and expected to fully perform our duties as husband and wife. In order to maintain a strong relationship, Christ must be at the center of the marriage. The earthly foundation of the family is built upon the strength of the husband and wife, mother and father, step mom and step dad.

In order for the blended family to function properly, the husband and wife must be strong and allow the Holy Spirit guide their marriage and relationships. It must be spirit led according to God's Word. It has to be bathed in expressions of love. Children need to observe the parents striving to do God's will and expressing love towards one another. Another vital element of a spirit guided relationship is following the instructions found in God's Word regarding the husband and wife.

WIVES:

What does the Bible say, concerning the role and responsibilities of the husband and wife? Below is scripture defining the role of each spouse. Let's look at what the Bible says in Ephesians chapter 5: verses 22–31 concerning the husband and wife.

Marriage, Christ and the Church

[22] Wives, submit to your own husbands, as to the Lord.

[23] For the husband is head of the wife, as also Christ is head of the church; and He is the Savior of the body.

[24] Therefore, just as the church is subject to Christ, so *let* the wives *be* to their own husbands in everything.

[25] Husbands, love your wives, just as Christ also loved the church and gave Himself for her,

[26] that He might sanctify and cleanse her with the washing of water by the word,

[27] that He might present her to Himself a glorious church, not having spot or wrinkle or any such thing, but that she should be holy and without blemish.

[28] So husbands ought to love their own wives as their own bodies; he who loves his wife loves himself.

[29] For no one ever hated his own flesh, but nourishes and cherishes it, just as the Lord *does* the church.

[30] For we are members of His body, of His flesh and of His bones.

[31] *"For this reason a man shall leave his father and mother and be joined to his wife, and the two shall become one flesh."*

1 *The New King James Version,* (Nashville, TN: Thomas Nelson Publishers) 1998, c1982

My wife Marie is a prime example.

HUSBANDS:

In the King James Version of the Bible, the word husband is mentioned 120 times, in 104 verses. Consider that for a moment, and you find yourself thinking of how important the husband is in the family. The Bible tells us that the husband is the head of the home, the spiritual leader, and the one who sets the example for the family. One of the main reasons for the deterioration of the American family today, is failure on the part of men, husbands, and fathers to carry out their God given responsibilities.

Without exception, husbands are to cherish and nurture the very flower God has seen fit to provide. . . . their wives. No wife is perfect, but neither are we. Men **must** be leaders in the home and church, carrying out their roles in such a way as God has ordered and ordained them.

Leaders in the Church:

As men we are required to seek the Lord and His righteousness, including being men of good standing and character. Men and their families should find a good church and become involved. I believe everyone has a talent and men who seek God, should use their talents for the building of His kingdom.

When we work in the church or work in a ministry that is a representation of the Christian faith, we should adhere to the guidelines found in 1st Timothy chapter three verses one through nine.

1st Timothy chapter 3: verses 1–9.

[1] This *is* a faithful saying: If a man desires the position of a bishop, he desires a good work.

[2] A bishop then must be blameless, the husband of one wife, temperate, sober-minded, of good
behavior, hospitable, able to teach;

[3] not given to wine, not violent, not greedy for money, but gentle, not quarrelsome, not covetous;

⁴ one who rules his own house well, having *his* children in submission with all reverence
⁵ (for if a man does not know how to rule his own house, how will he take care of the church of God?);
⁶ not a novice, lest being puffed up with pride he fall into the *same* condemnation as the devil.
⁷ Moreover he must have a good testimony among those who are outside, lest he fall into reproach and the snare of the devil.
⁸ Likewise deacons *must be* reverent, not double-tongued, not given to much wine, not greedy for money,
⁹ holding the mystery of the faith with a pure conscience.
The New King James Version, (Nashville, TN: Thomas Nelson Publishers) 1998, c1982

We may not be called as Pastors, called into full time ministry, or selected as Deacons, etc, but what we are called to do is live a life according to the guidelines you just read and live a Christ centered life before our family and others. In essence we are evangelists in our homes, workplace and anywhere we go, spreading the Gospel of Christ and sharing the good news. What better calling than to minister to *all* people, especially our family.

Remember it starts in the home, with the husband and father.

As we just read, men have an awesome responsibility as the leader in the home and in the church. The instruction is explicit and to the point. Imagine family life in America today if every husband patterned his life after 1ˢᵗ Timothy 3, 1–9, on a regular basis.

Men are required to provide spiritual, emotional and financial stability for their families. The wife and children need a husbands, a fathers and step fathers support more than we will ever know. Consider the benefits of a Christ centered family as opposed to one built upon the foundation of this world. It doesn't take long to see the difference. There are many ways in which we can accomplish this.

The following scriptures are guidelines for all men, especially dads and step dads.

Prov 9:9 Instruct a wise man and he will be wiser still; teach a righteous man and he will add to his learning.

Prov 10:4 Lazy hands make a man poor, but diligent hands bring wealth.

Prov 10:9 The man of integrity walks securely, but he who takes crooked paths will be found out.

Prov 11:17–20 A kind man benefits himself, but a cruel man brings trouble on himself. [18] The wicked man earns deceptive wages, but he who sows righteousness reaps a sure reward. [19] The truly righteous man attains life, but he who pursues evil goes to his death. [20] The LORD detests men of perverse heart but he delights in those whose ways are blameless.

Matt 5:16 In the same way, let your light shine before men, that they may see your good deeds and praise your Father in heaven.

Matt 6:14 For if you forgive men when they sin against you, your heavenly Father will also forgive you.

The New International Version ® *1973, 1978, 1984*

I once read a list of 25 ways to spiritually lead your wife from a well known expert on the family. As I began a new family with my new wife, I learned a lot of the same things and by the way, I'm still learning today.

Based on my experience, I have developed a top 20 list of things men can do to spiritually lead their wives. Are you the spiritual leader in your home?

THE TOP 20 LIST OF THINGS MEN CAN DO TO SPIRITUALLY LEAD THEIR WIVES AND FAMILIES:

1. Begin your day with your wife on your mind and be thankful that she is yours.
2. Leave a mushy post-it note (several of them) in conspicuous locations for her to find.
3. Read the Bible and discuss God's Word with her.
4. Kneel down with your wife; pray and humble yourself before God.
5. Take your wife for a walk in the park or mall.
6. Don't be afraid to show your wife affection. (This includes the children as well.)
7. Get to know your wife's needs, wants and desires. (Let her know that you are concerned for her well being.)
8. Focus on the talents and abilities your wife has. Tell your wife (in private and in front of others) that she is good at what she does. (a wonderful wife, mother, step mom, etc) Brag on her whenever you get the chance.
9. Honor your marriage and your wife. Remain committed to her . . . always.
10. Focus on your wife's beauty and not someone else's. Tell her she looks beautiful; go as far to say she looks sexy.
11. Do something spontaneous and unexpected for your wife.
12. Walk the talk in front of your wife and family. Let the family know the importance of serving God through a relationship with Christ. Live and practice what you preach.
13. Treat her kids as your kids. Love on them as you would your own.
14. Be open to the needs of the family and listen to what they have to say. You may be surprised what you learn.
15. Pray with the kids. It works!

16. Correct and discipline the children with love, treating everyone the same. (yours and hers)
17. Develop obtainable goals, objectives and priorities for the blended family.
18. Reward and praise when family members do well. (accomplish a goal, do good in school, or church, stand up against peer pressure, etc.)
19. Set aside special family times
20. Persevere and don't quit.

1a. Do you think all, or part of the 20 items you just read are part of your daily routine regarding the relationship with your wife and family?

O YES   O NO

1.b If you checked no to the above question, then what steps do you need to take, or changes do you need to make, in order for you to reach your goal of all 20?

Write your answer in the space provided below.

_____
_____
_____
_____
_____

2. What does the Bible say concerning a husband's responsibility in marriage and the way he should treat his wife?

_____
_____
_____
_____
_____

3. What does God expect of the man in a marriage and being a spiritual leader in the church?

_____

_____

_____

_____

_____

WIVES:

Nothing is more precious than a wife who seeks to follow God and do His will. Talk about the backbone of an organization; you have it with a wife and mother. I have seen time and time again, that wives who seek to follow Christ and remain faithful, are the backbone of the earthly family. Women, especially wives and mothers have what I call

"The Resiliency Factor" working in their life.

As I was writing Building a Blended Family I thought of a word that describes my wife in regards to the challenges she faced early in our journey together as we attempted to stitch together our new family. The word. . . . resilience! Then I thought of the "The Resiliency Factor."

Let's look at the definition for the word resilient. Webster defines resilient as " . . . the ability to bounce back." My wife and so many others have a unique and unusual way of facing adversity and bouncing back from the trials and tribulations of married life in a blended family setting. Their God-given ability to stand strong throughout adversity stands as a monument to the character of a godly wife.

In the Bible (King James Version) the word wives is mentioned 133 times. This indicates how important the wife is to her husband and family. A good wife is beneficial to a man and shows God's favor on him. As I mentioned, God has given women a natural urge to bounce back from any type of adversity. It amazes me to see the strength most women have and their ability to love. What a prime example of the love Christ has for His children.

What does the Bible say about the wife and her role in the family?

Proverbs 31:10–30:
A Wife of Noble Character

10 Who can find a virtuous and capable wife? She is worth more than precious rubies.

11 Her husband can trust her, and she will greatly enrich his life.

12 She will not hinder him but help him all her life.

13 She finds wool and flax and busily spins it.

14 She is like a merchant's ship; she brings her food from afar.

15 She gets up before dawn to prepare breakfast for her household and plan the day's work for her servant girls.

16 She goes out to inspect a field and buys it; with her earnings she plants a vineyard.

17 She is energetic and strong, a hard worker.

18 She watches for bargains; her lights burn late into the night.

19 Her hands are busy spinning thread, her fingers twisting fiber.

20 She extends a helping hand to the poor and opens her arms to the needy.

21 She has no fear of winter for her household because all of them have warm clothes.

22 She quilts her own bedspreads. She dresses like royalty in gowns of finest cloth.

23 Her husband is well known, for he sits in the council meeting with the other civic leaders.

24 She makes belted linen garments and sashes to sell to the merchants.

25 She is clothed with strength and dignity, and she laughs with no fear of the future.

²⁶ When she speaks, her words are wise, and kindness is the rule when she gives instructions.

²⁷ She carefully watches all that goes on in her household and does not have to bear the consequences of laziness.

²⁸ Her children stand and bless her. Her husband praises her:

²⁹ "There are many virtuous and capable women in the world, but you surpass them all!"

³⁰ Charm is deceptive, and beauty does not last; but a woman who fears the Lord will be greatly praised.

³¹ Reward her for all she has done. Let her deeds publicly declare her praise.

Holy Bible, New Living Translation,
(Wheaton, IL: Tyndale House Publishers, Inc.) 1996

1st Corinthians 7:14

¹⁴ For the Christian wife brings holiness to her marriage, and the Christian husband brings holiness to his marriage. Otherwise, your children would not have a godly influence. *New Living Translation,* (Wheaton, IL: Tyndale House Publishers, Inc.) 1996

Colossians 3:18 and 19:

¹⁸ You wives must submit to your husbands, as is fitting for those who belong to the Lord.

¹⁹ And you husbands must love your wives and never treat them harshly. *New Living Translation,* (Wheaton, IL: Tyndale House Publishers, Inc.) 1996

1st Peter 3:1, 2 and 7

In the same way, you wives must accept the authority of your husbands, even those who refuse to accept the Good News. Your godly lives will speak to them better than any words. They will be won over [2] by watching your pure, godly behavior. [7] In the same way, you husbands must give honor to your wives. Treat her with understanding as you live together. She may be weaker than you are, but she is your equal partner in God's gift of new life. If you don't treat her as you should, your prayers will not be heard. *New Living Translation,* (Wheaton, IL: Tyndale House Publishers, Inc.) 1996

It is so important for husbands and wives to follow God's commands concerning their roles as husband and wife. Doing so pleases God and makes for a happier, healthier and more joyful life, not to mention the impact on the family as a whole.

Earlier, I gave you my Top 20 List of Things Men Can do to Spiritually Lead Their Wives and Families. Below is my wife's list entitled "The Top 20 List of Things Women Can do to Make Their Husbands a Strong Spiritual Leader."

Review the list below carefully.

You may find more than one item on the list that needs to be changed, improved, or added in your life.

THE TOP 20 LIST OF THINGS WOMEN CAN DO TO MAKE THEIR HUSBANDS A STRONG SPIRITUAL LEADER:

1. Begin your day with your husband on your mind and be thankful he is yours.
2. Leave a "sweetie post it note" (several of them) in conspicuous locations for him to find.
3. Read the Bible and discuss God's word with him.
4. Ask your husband to pray with you. Let him know how important it is to you that he be the spiritual leader in the home.
5. Ask your husband to take you for a walk in the park or

mall. Let him know you just want to spend some special time alone with him.

6. Don't be afraid to show your husband some affection.
7. Find out your husband needs and wants. (let him know that you are concerned for his well being)
8. Focus on the talents and abilities your husband has. Tell him in private and in front of others that he is good at what he does and how wonderful a father he is. Brag on him whenever you get the chance.)
9. Honor your marriage and your husband. Remain committed to him . . . always.
10. Focus on your husband's good looks and not someone else's. Tell him that he looks good and is very handsome. (You can go as far to say that he looks sexy.)
11. Do something spontaneous and unexpected for your husband.
12. Walk the life of a Christ-serving wife in front of your husband and family.
13. Treat his kids as your kids. Love on them as you would your own.
14. Be open to the needs of your husband and family. Listen to what they have to say.
15. If you have children, pray with them (his and yours). It works!
16. Correct and discipline the children with love, treating everyone the same. (yours and his)
17. Develop obtainable goals, objectives and priorities for yourself and your husband.
18. Set aside special family times. This includes your husband as well.
19. Practice what you preach and teach; always.
20. Persevere and don't quit.

Take a moment to consider and discuss the following questions:

BUILDING A BLENDED FAMILY

1a. Do you think all 20 items you just read are part of your daily routine in relationship on how you treat your husband and family?

O YES   O NO

1b. If you checked no to the above question, then what steps do you need to take, or changes do you need to make, in order for you to reach your goal of all 20?

Write your answer in the space provided below.

_____
_____
_____
_____
_____

2. a. What does the Bible say concerning a husband's responsibility in marriage and the way he should treat his wife?

_____
_____
_____
_____

b. What does the Bible say concerning a wife's responsibility in marriage and the way she should treat her husband?

_____
_____
_____
_____
_____

3. What does God expect of the husband and wife in marriage?

_____
_____

_____

_____

_____

FIVE WAYS TO BETTER ENHANCE A
BLENDED FAMILY MARRIAGE:

People ask me over and over, "Phil, how can I better enhance the relationship with my spouse?" I respond without hesitation, "In my own marriage I have to work daily at keeping it strong." Everyday presents unexpected challenges. Focusing on God, reading His word, and a personal relationship with Jesus Christ are the key elements in a loving marriage and a lasting marriage with fulfillment.

Working with many blended families and talking with family counselors, I've found five key elements necessary in keeping a blended family marriage in check and in balance.

Follow the guidelines listed below and you will be amazed at the transformation that can and will take place in your marriage and blended family life.

1. HUSBANDS AND WIVES NEED TO
TALK TO ONE ANOTHER:

Communication is one of the most valuable aspects of a healthy marriage without exception. I've met hundred's of couples who struggle with keeping their thoughts and feelings to themselves, only discovering later that their failure to communicate leads to anger, resentfulness, bitterness, unforgiveness and no communication at all.

So many couples in blended family relationships hide their emotions from each other, as a result of low self-esteem, hidden issues from a previous marriage, or the way they were raised by their parents. Hidden or unresolved issues can lead to confusion and conflict within the blended family setting.

Understand that when spouses fail to communicate and listen to one another, eventually one or both may seek out someone who will. Failure to communicate sends a spouse down the hallway that leads to the door of temptation.

Let's look at the following example:

Imagine you're having a rough time at work, and the past several weeks have been really hard. You've tried on several occasions to talk to your spouse about what is happening, but he or she refuse to listen and appears concerned with other things that seem more important.

You go to work the next day and from nowhere this attractive person enters your office and says . . . you seem worried and stressed out. What's wrong, can I help?" You proceed to explain your situation; the person listens with an attentive heart and is very concerned. All of a sudden he or she speaks the words that open the door to temptation, "You know, I can relate to what you're saying. I feel the same way; my spouse doesn't care or listen to me either and also seems preoccupied with things more important than me.

This person walks away, turns, stops, looks back, and says, "Let's do lunch tomorrow; I'll come by your office and pick you up." You just connected with a person who seems to care about your feelings and needs. This person relates to your pain. The door to temptation just opened, and a seed to personal and family destruction has been planted. Will the seed grow? *Once the door to temptation is cracked opened, it becomes harder to close.*

The scenario you just read, takes place countless number of times everyday in our country. In so many cases the lives of men and women, including innocent family members are destroyed. Connect with your spouse, communicate, don't turn your back, listen, pray, and read God's Word together. Take time to discuss the things that bother you, or your spouse.

The key to resisting temptation is through the study of God's word, prayer, and a determination to resist. James 4:7 tells us, "Therefore submit yourselves to God; resist the devil and he shall flee."

Notice that it doesn't say he might, or probably will flee, it specifically states that *he will flee,* period without exception.

In Proverbs 4:23 we are told to guard our heart because it guides us in everything we do. Proverbs 4:24 tells to avoid perverse talk and stay away from corrupt speech. It's amazing how just a few spoken words can affect us for a lifetime, if we aren't careful.

Read the following scripture.
1st Corinthians 10:13:

[13] No temptation has overtaken you except such as is common to man; but God *is* faithful, who will not allow you to be tempted beyond what you are able, but with the temptation will also make the way of escape, that you may be able to bear it. *The New King James Version,* (Nashville, TN: Thomas Nelson Publishers) 1998, c1982

2. GUARD YOUR HEART SO JEALOUSY DOESN'T TAKE OVER.

They say money is the root of all evil. Would you believe that jealousy is the root of many divorces and problems in marriages today? It's true that many spouses have been frustrated by the other half's failure to provide the necessary attention they need and deserve, or the way a spouse may show his or her affection to someone else, or something else; a job, a hobby, sport, friends, etc. So many times when jealousy pays us a visit, we make sarcastic remarks, or unnecessary comments, usually making us look foolish, or just plain **STUPID**. Don't allow jealousy to control you.

James 3:15 - 17 tells us. . . . .

[15] For jealousy and selfishness are not God's kind of wisdom. Such things are earthly, unspiritual, and motivated by the Devil. *New Living Translation,* (Wheaton, IL: Tyndale House Publishers, Inc.) 1996

[16] For wherever there is jealousy and selfish ambition, there you will find disorder and every kind of evil. *New Living Translation,* (Wheaton, IL: Tyndale House Publishers, Inc.) 1996

Now the opposite of jealousy is WISDOM and it shall prevail. Verse 17 gives us the purpose and reason for seeking wisdom no matter what we face in life.

[17] But the wisdom that comes from heaven is first of all pure. It is also peace loving, gentle at all times, and willing to yield to others. It is full of mercy and good deeds. It shows no partiality and is always sincere. *New Living Translation,* (Wheaton, IL: Tyndale House Publishers, Inc.) 1996

If you ever become jealous, seek God for direction, talk with your spouse to express your feelings and find out the source(s) of any jealousy. Be prepared to ask for forgiveness and if necessary, forgive. **Do not allow** the seeds of jealousy to grow into a bush cluttered with thorns that can cut deep into the emotions and affect the relationship between you and your spouse.

3. ENJOY YOUR SPOUSE.

I want to be appreciated and feel very good when my wife lets me know that she does appreciate what I do for her and the family. I have no doubt that you feel the same way too. I once read that when we sincerely put forth the effort to show that we love the one we are married too, three things happen:

1. **We honor God by showing love and adhering to His Word.**
2. **We lift up and give our spouse confidence.**
3. **We are reminded of what an awesome spouse we have.**

That is so true because no husband or wife is perfect, we can't expect our spouse to be Mr. America / Miss America, or Mr. Cleaver / Mrs. Cleaver (Remember Leave it to Beaver?) all the time. Lets accept one another for who we are and the way God made us. Spouses should give each other a compliment everyday and compliment one another when in public as well. **Compliments build and polish our self-esteem.**

The husband and wife must position themselves correctly in the home, one with another before the rest of the family functions properly.

4. BECOME AN ACCOUNTABILITY PARTNER WITH YOUR SPOUSE:

Blended families, the husband and wife, and the parents need to get involved in a church, a small group, or anything that would hold them biblically accountable for their marriage and family.

God uses the church and its members as tools to assist the husband and wife in remaining completely accountable to one another. Ground your family in a strong Bible believing church and seek out strong Christian friends who will allow you to be honest about your marriage and family. True Christian friends and family will support you, pray for you / with you, your spouse and family. True Christian friends help us overcome many of the temptations we face in life as married couples in blended family environments and keep the accountability process in check.

5. PRAY AND FAST:

Without a doubt, the key to a successful marriage and blended family relationship is seeking God through prayer, fasting and the study of His word. As I mentioned earlier, resisting temptation is one of the major keys to a successful marriage and a secure family life. It sets the tone for dealing with problems that might arise in our families. How do we do this?

The answer is simple:
1. **Submit to God completely.**
2. **Study God's Word.**
3. **Communicate with your spouse.**
4. **Let your spouse know you appreciate them.**
5. **PRAY and set aside a time to fast for God's direction in your life.**

Prayer is the switch that throws the main breaker, releasing the power for effective Christian living. Families need to exercise this God given command daily. Praying and seeking God is the answer to building a strong blended family foundation. God will bless our faithfulness. In the end, it is up to us to choose and do what is right. I find comfort in knowing I'm not alone when tempted, tested, or facing family trials, etc.

God is faithful and His promises keep us safe from the things of this world.

1. Have you experienced any temptation recently?

O YES   O NO

If you answered yes, what steps will you take in resisting the temptation?

_____

_____

_____

_____

2. Have you prayed with your spouse recently?

    O YES   O NO

If no, write down the things you feel are hindering you from praying with your spouse.

_____

_____

_____

_____

3. Do you communicate with your spouse the way you should?

    O YES   O NO

If no, what will you do to improve communication between you and your spouse?

_____

_____

_____

_____

CHAPTER 4

God's Plan for
the Mother and Father:

The mother and father are key players in shaping the character of a young child. In this chapter I want to discuss the role of the mother and father.

MOTHERS:

What does the Bible say about mothers?

Proverbs 31:25–28 describes a mother as one who "is clothed with strength and dignity; she can laugh at the days to come. She speaks with wisdom and faithful instruction is on her tongue. She watches over the affairs of her household and does not eat the bread of idleness. Her children arise and call her blessed."

A mother and wife shouldn't have to nag, or raise her voice constantly in order for the kids or even her husband to listen to her. Moms worry about the things that are important, for example: Are the dishes done? Are there any plates/cups lying around in places they shouldn't be? Are clothes lying on the floor, or hanging on the end of the bed? My wife is a stickler when it comes to keeping the house clean—what a blessing! By the way men must do their part in keeping things clean as well.

Not only does a good mother need good housekeeping habits, she also needs to exercise proper speech as well. My mom use to say, "When I was your age, kids had it much harder. My mother didn't take me anywhere. . . ."

I did hear my mother say that from time to time, and you know she had the right because at times, I did take her and all she did for me for granted.

I once read that Mothers can belt out the national anthem of motherhood regardless of the indifference of the crowd. She can make herself heard over a blaring television set, a CD player, or teenagers talking on a telephone. I guess God made mothers that way.

My wife, Marie, is a wonderful mother and step-mother. She works full-time, takes care of the home, and still finds time to help others outside the home and in church. She cooks, cleans, and launders without expecting to be appreciated. In today's family, most children have lost the directions to the laundry room and would be content to eat off paper plates or pizza boxes for the rest of their lives.

Work on your children, train them, we do.

A good mother, like my wife, is more than just a cook, cleaning lady, and one who takes our clothes to the laundry, or goes to the drug store, she is a mom, director, my best friend, my wife. My biological son refers to his step mom as simply "Mom." What a compliment for a wife in a blended family relationship. A mother (a mom) has a heart for the hurting and she has a soft lap for our grandchildren. She can be hardheaded about discipline (especially compared with "everyone else's mother") and softhearted about everything else.

A good mother and step mother is charged to give her children and stepchildren more than a balanced diet and a roof over their heads. She is a teacher, who instructs the children on how to feed their souls and gives them a firm spiritual foundation on which to build their lives. A good mom / step mom prays for her children making sure they stay on the proper path in life. A mother, a step mother shows love by praying for children and step children unconditionally.

I often wonder if God created mothers because He needed someone to keep every generation reminded of His presence. Good mothers have been doing that for thousands of years, ever since Eve held her first born.

As important as mothers are to us, it is amazing how often we take them for granted. Mother's Day is a good time to show appreciation and honor our mothers / stepmoms. They shall be called blessed. Don't wait until Mother's Day to show appreciation; do it today.

I believe what the Bible says about mothers applies to stepmothers to. There are many children in blended families whose only mother figure is their stepmom; what an opportunity a stepmother has to mold the life of a child. A stepmother may very well be the saving grace in a stepchild's life. I know this all to well; my wife has made a tremendous difference in my oldest daughter's life. God used my wife to perform a mighty work in my daughter's life and rescue her from potential emotional destruction.

In chapter 11 you will read the miraculous story of my daughter Jenna.

I often wondered if it was true when people said there was a difference between a mother and a mom. I can say from experience that there is. Just look at my wife; she is a mom, a good mom.

FATHERS:

So often fathers do not receive the attention and recognition they deserve. It has been said that fatherhood is and should be the cornerstone of the American family. Through their actions, deeds, and words, a father can have an immeasurable impact on the life of his wife, his biological children, step children and others.

What separates a father from a great father? Martin Luther King III, president of the Southern Christian Leadership Conference once said, "Daddy preached in church many of the same lessons that we learned at home. First and foremost, we were taught the 'Golden Rule'—that one should treat your fellow human being as you would want to be treated. In addition to that, we were taught to honor our parents and to love our neighbors. The greatest commodity in our home was love."

A great father doesn't have to be rich, famous, powerful, or an intellectual genius. All he needs to succeed in life is to seek and strive to serve God, to do the small things.

Fathers and stepfathers (dads) just need to be there for the family, to be a role model and pillar of strength, a seeker of truth, a provider, someone who loves his wife and encourages his children to strive for the best above all the rest and then settle for nothing less.

Being a great father is about instilling wisdom, strength, and the right values in an impressionable child before someone else is successful in instilling the wrong values.

Many well known individuals have been blessed to have had great fathers or father figures in their lives. Perhaps the most important lesson we can learn from the great fathers of yesteryear and history is that fatherhood is not a popularity contest. Being a father / dad is a self-fulfilling, and may be the most rewarding position a man could ever have. Nothing is more rewarding than to know that a father can help mold, shape, and change the life of a child for the good. Many children in a blended family relationship have no biological fathers in their lives. What an awesome opportunity for the "stepfather" or shall I say **DAD** to make a difference for the rest of their lives.

Remember . . . . . . .Any man can be a father, but it takes a real man to be a dad.

QUESTIONS TO CONSIDER:

1. Are you being the mother and father God wants you to be and must be?

O YES   O NO

2. If you answered no, then what steps do you need to take in order to get into compliance with God's Word? Write your answers below.

_____

_____

_____

_____

_____

CHAPTER 5

The Blended Family

As I mentioned earlier, the blended family is fast becoming the largest family group in America. The blended family encounters obstacles of a different kind than those faced by the nuclear or traditional family. Some of those challenges include jealousy, disruption by the ex-spouse, children, loyalty issues, discipline concerns, favoritism parenting issues, etc. Trying to build a blended family is a challenge. Hard work and preparation is required in the building process. Let's look at the truth verses hearsay regarding blended family life.

As a husband and father in a blended family, I found it very important to do things together in order to keep the family strong. A strong blended family makes family members even stronger. Strength in the blended family comes from a close walk with God by both parents. It is the glue that holds the family together.

As you will read, married couples in a blended family setting, face certain specific challenges that no other family group faces, and spending quality time with your spouse is so important. It is very important to schedule time for you and your spouse. Go on a date on a regular basis or just go some where and "hang out" alone!

Discipline is so important in the family, especially the blended family. Fathers, stepfathers, mothers and stepmothers can provide stability and leadership in the blended family by seeking God for direction in managing the family properly.

Discipline is dealt with authority and unity from the husband and wife.

Anger and dissension between couples over discipline and other issues should be discussed privately. Learn to agree and to disagree without creating separation in the family. Seek God and pray when issues arise that create conflict.

All members of the blended family must know and understand their roles in the family. Love, discipline and structure are very important in keeping a blended family together. Reward children for completing chores and be consistent in administering consequences for not completing chores and required duties.

The husband and wife should decide on disciplinary protocol and the methods of administering discipline. The biological parent should generally administer the disciplinary action. In the event the biological parent is absent, the stepparent needs to be firm in reminding the child of disciplinary action. When administering discipline, be very careful *not* to put the child down, thereby keeping the child's self-esteem intact.

Many children in a blended family will expressively speak their minds in a very negative way concerning how they feel in their new family situation. One of my greatest struggles in building our family was battling the feelings and emotions my step sons (now my adopted sons) had in the early phases of my marriage to their mother.

There are children who keep their feelings and emotions hidden until something happens, or a situation occurs that reminds them of their past. Many children act out their feelings through disrespect and rebellion. Both the biological parent and stepparent should speak to the children about their feelings, fears, and concerns. Never assume all is well with the emotional stability of your child. **You may be surprised at the storm that rages within them.**

When problems occur in the blended family, take time to

locate the problem and determine if the problem is attributed to the blended family setting or related to something else. Work out the problem together. Have family meetings and discuss the feelings of each party involved. Don't be afraid to ask, "What's wrong?"

If we assume that developing and building a blended family were an easy task, then we need to think again. Imagine entering into a marriage with seven children as I did. My wife's children had never had a relationship with their biological father; therefore I assumed my wife's children would accept me with open arms. It didn't take long for me to find out just how wrong I was.

Through experience and study of other blended families, I have learned that there are several assumptions individuals make when entering into a relationship or marriage that forms a blended family.

1. Assuming there will be an automatic "love connection" between children and stepparents.

In most cases it takes time to develop a good relationship with stepchildren. Like with adults, children need time to get to know their new family members, especially step parents. Trust is very important to children. A common belief by children is that their new step mom, or step dad took their mom or dad from them and caused the divorce of their biological parents. Taking time to get to know one another and being who you are is crucial in the early stages of a new blended family.

2. Assuming that children of divorce and remarriage are emotionally damaged forever.

Believe it or not, children of divorce and remarriage go through moments and seasons of adjustment, including grief. Many believe that children are very resilient and the parents need more help then they do during times of separation, divorce, and remarriage. Wrong! It is imperative that biological parents, stepparents, and family members work with the children of divorce and blended families.

I encourage you to listen as children express their feelings, concerns, disappointments, and hurts as you build your new family.

Life changes can make or break a child emotionally. Children need structure and discipline to help keep their emotions in check, which assists in creating a well-balanced individual able to handle future challenges they will face in life.

After my separation and divorce, I thought I needed to do special things and buy special things for my children, in an attempt to "make it up to my kids" for the divorce they had to go through. Trying to "make it up to the children" results in complicating matters when attempting to respond appropriately to their hurts and emotions. It also hampers a parent's ability when attempting to set appropriate boundaries for their children which is a vital and an important part of parenting.

Children are strong, yet what they need more than anything else is love, a shoulder to lean on and a parent, or step parent who will take the time and listen to them. As the old song goes, "all I need is love. Feeling loved and understood is a very important part of a child's well being and emotional development. It is a necessity in building a blended family setting.

3. Assuming that stepmothers and stepfathers are evil people.

Negative perceptions of stepmothers and stepfathers are commonplace occurrences in blended families. These perceptions also exist within the general public as well. Inappropriate perceptions of stepparents impacts children in a negative way, especially in the early days of blended family development. Many stepmothers and stepfathers become over-achievers (like myself) and work too hard at making things perfect for the new blended family, which in reality only complicates matters and makes the adjustment process more difficult.

It is not uncommon to find stepparents being the ones who end having a more difficult time during early stages of blended family life. Many stepmothers and stepfathers provide more stability and emotional security than a child's own biological parents who may, or may not be in the picture. Stepparents are individuals just like the biological parents and should have the children's best interest at hand.

4. Assuming that a blended family will connect without any problems.

Wouldn't it be wonderful if this were true? I can tell you from experience that it takes time and effort for a blended family to connect and it will not happen overnight. When an individual marries and begins, or becomes part of a blended family there is and should be excitement, however when the honeymoon period levels out, be prepared for unexpected changes.

Let's face it; it takes four to seven years for a new family to develop its on roots and take hold. Statistics indicate that individuals who remarry and the marriage forms a blended family/ stepfamily will divorce within three years. It takes time for people to get to know each other, create positive relationships, and develop some family history. Read, pray, communicate, attend church, and make friends with other blended families. **It's worth it!**

5. Assuming that children will have an easier time adjusting to blended family life if the biological mother or father is not in the picture.

WRONG! How far from the truth could this be. More than ever children need their biological parents in the picture.

Face reality; biological parents are part of blended family life—like it or not, dead or alive. Issues such as when to get the kids for the holidays or family events, involvement with school programs, sporting events, where to take the children to meet their mother or father, etc, are all part of the blended family no matter how you look at it, or how much you may dislike it.

Let us not forget contact between the new spouse and his, or her old spouse may occur. Try to open, create and maintain channels of communication between you and your ex-spouse. This will help to eliminate and or reduce any potential conflict. There are cases where the biological parent may not or should not be in the picture, but rest assured that dead or alive, children still have strong connections with their biological parents.

If you believe that the absence or removing a biological parent from the equation of the blended family life always makes things easier, read very carefully the following true story of what occurred 4 years after my wife and I married.

It was during the day on February 26th, 2002 when my wife received a phone call that would impact her and her children for months and years to come. She received a call informing her that her ex-husband was tragically killed in an automobile accident. When I first heard the news, my initial reaction and concern was how would the boys react to their father's death?

But then again I thought, "Okay, no big deal here the kids haven't seen their dad and really don't even know him; they won't be to upset." Was I mistaken? Little did I know or ever expect what I was about to see.

Of my four adopted sons, my youngest adopted son (Shane) who didn't even know his real father reacted very surprisingly. His emotions sky-rocketed and I saw expressions of grief and pain that caught me by surprise. Would you believe I got angry at his outward expressions? I became selfish, and for days I continually asked myself and even made the comment to my wife, "How could Shane be so upset? I'm his dad; I've done more for him in two years than his real father did during his life time."

My wife even cried during this time of loss. At first I thought, could she still be in love with her ex husband? I soon learned that her tears and sadness were not expressions of love towards her ex, but concern and hurt for her children and the loss of their father.

You see, I wanted all of Shane's love. I was selfish and didn't care about his feelings, only mine. I soon learned the importance of being sensitive to the feelings of a child, especially when they've lost, or are losing contact with their biological parent(s). I also learned how powerful the "biological connection" (as I call it) is, no matter how close or far away a parent may be. Stepparents / adopted parents must be available and open to communicate with their stepchildren at a moments notice. One of the fastest ways to earn trust and respect is letting your stepchild know that you are there for them.

The truth is that in most cases children will always have (for the majority of their life) two biological parents, but in the unfortunate event they lose one, be prepared and available to assist in anyway you can. Put yourself in their shoes.

6. Assuming good relationships will occur between the non-custodial parent:

It is true that for the most part children adjust better to blended family relationships when their biological parents are in the picture and *getting along*. There are times however when visitation by the non-custodial parent creates problems as well. Just be prepared and exercise humility. Yes humility, because there may be a time when you have to humble yourself and be the adult when a non-custodial crosses the line.

Good relationships are important between the ex-spouse and or the non-custodial parent. In the event of situations where ex-spouses or non-custodial parents are at odds, it is important to a child's emotional health and well being that they see someone exercising restraint concerning the situation at hand. It also teaches children how to act under stressful situations. It is important to use caution and be prepared when dealing with difficult non-custodial parents.

It is a vital necessity and in the best interest of the children that the biological parent and stepparent work at developing strategies for dealing with difficult non-custodial parents. Success may not occur overnight, but the long term benefits are priceless.

7. Underestimating the bond between your spouse and their children.

Before a single parent marries, careful consideration must be taken regarding the emotions, feelings, and bond that have developed with children living in a single parent home. Single parent families develop their own standards, methods of conduct, and methods of communicating. The longer children live with a single parent, the more likely they are to develop a strong foundation built around the parent with whom they live. There is nothing wrong with this; the couple just needs to be prepared to deal with some unexpected emotions and attitudes from their child / children when their lifestyle changes as a result of remarriage.

Failure to understand the bond between a single parent and the child creates a gateway to conflict. Jealously, anger, resentment, even hatred can be birthed into children who may feel left out, or uninvolved by your new spouse and his, or her children.

I can relate to this particular conflict. It happened to me, and the emotions created by underestimating the bond between my wife and her sons were an unexpected trial. I assumed all would be fine especially since my wife's children had no contact with their biological father. I was so wrong

I soon learned that if I were not careful, resentment, anxiety, jealousy, indifference or dislike for my wife's children could occur. Don't get me wrong, negative feelings are perfectly normal but at times, are difficult to admit and still more difficult to face. In cases like this, it is so important to seek God for direction.

8. Assuming there will be no disciplinary issues in your blended family!

Well here is another **WRONG!** The truth about discipline is that you can't do it alone in a blended family relationship. This issue causes many problems, especially during the early stages of blended family life. Many children, especially teens, will resist any attempt by a stepparent to discipline when and if necessary.

The anger and frustration that results when disciplinary measures are required, can cause immediate division among your new blended family if you are not careful. Division in the family should be *unacceptable!!* Newly married couples (even couples planning to marry) in a newly formed blended family need to talk and prepare an action plan on how disciplinary protocol will be carried out in the event it becomes necessary.

Developing house rules and having the biological parent enforce the rules and consequences is highly recommended in the early stages of a blended family. In my case, I attempted to be the rule maker and disciplinarian from the day my wife and I married. Again I learned something very quickly; you can't always do what you think you can. Go slow, plan, discuss disciplinary action with your spouse and take your time!

When you assume the role of a newly wed husband or wife and stepparent without prior and proper counseling by a professional, discussion, planning and agreement with your spouse-to-be, you will be caught off guard and conflict will arise. . .guaranteed.

Even the best planned, frequently discussed, and properly developed action plans can meet resistance. Be prepared, seek God for direction, do not be afraid to ask for help and. . . pray!

If we fail to address even the smallest of issues or problems, they tend to form walls of resentment over time within the blended family. The smallest of problems can also form

mountains of conflict leading to dissention and the destruction of a blended family.

Be aware of the emotional landmines that family members can step on engaging the mechanism that triggers an explosion of conflict and dissention...

EMOTIONAL LANDMINES

During times of war, landmines have been used to surprise and kill enemy forces. Landmines are hidden explosive devices used catch the enemy off guard and render bodily harm, even death. Landmines are extremely lethal, dangerous and difficult to see because they are hidden just below the surface of the ground and go unnoticed.

The first line of defense against a landmine is to locate it, mark it, determine what type of landmine it is and disarm it. Marking and identifying the emotional landmines planted beneath your family's emotional surface allows you to take action and disarm it before it explodes.

There are several emotional landmines that I found exist in many blended family relationships, including mine. Here are the top five:

(1) UNFORGIVENESS, BITTERNESS, ANGER,
    HATRED-all wrapped up in one
(2) Verbal hurts as a result of harsh words spoken
(3) Children who carry baggage that goes unrecognized
(4) Competition
(5) Failure to understand and listen to a family member

Family members, especially children want to be heard, listened too, and understood by their parents and adults. When building a blended family, we as adults must try to learn to speak the same language so we can relate to the children. As one experienced in this area, the best advice I can offer as a parent, stepparent and adoptive parent, is try not to become overly sensitive about what some other family member may say.

Learn to remove yourself from conflict when and if conflict erupts as a result of something said by a blended family member, a stepchild, a biological child, an ex-spouse, or whomever. We are accountable for our words and actions. Left uncorrected we will have to stand before God one day and give an explanation as to why we did what we did, or why we didn't do what we should have done. Locate your family's landmines and disarm them before they explode.

VERBAL HURTS

Words can affect people in different ways, especially words spoken out of frustration in the early stages of blended family life. Parents and step parents must be very careful and cautious in what they say and how they say it. At times I opened my "big mouth" and spoke before I thought. I learned very quickly that I needed to think before I spoke and to exercise compassion and patience for those in my new family.

My father taught me to use wisdom and show love towards others when I may not understand their feelings or opinions. When communicating to members of a blended family, express love, compassion, understanding and listen to what they have to save. You never know what you might learn. Read the following scriptures. Do you need to apply these words of wisdom to your life?

Proverbs 10:31, 32 -
[31] The godly person gives wise advice, but the tongue that deceives will be cut off.
[32] The godly speak words that are helpful, but the wicked speak only what is corrupt.4

Proverbs 15:23, and 31
[23] Everyone enjoys a fitting reply; it is wonderful to say the right thing at the right time!

³¹ If you listen to constructive criticism, you will be at homeamong the wise.

Holy Bible, New Living Translation,

CHILDREN CARRY BAGGAGE TOO

I discovered early on that parents in a blended family are not the only ones bringing emotional baggage to a new family. In fact, children carry baggage too and are less likely to handle the transition in a new blended family environment as well as parents do. Try and help your children understand that a new family means you have to find a new place in that family.

Circumstances and relationships aren't the same as they were before. Reassure the children that they will be ok and are accepted. Communicating words of security are very important and a necessity. Feeling lost in a family is one of the worst things a child can feel. Emotional and family security goes a long way toward building a strong blended family.

Remember. . . . ."It's not their fault "

One of the largest and most explosive landmines to watch out for in a blended family is the child who blames themselves for a parent's previous divorce or events leading to the separation and divorce of the parent. In many divorces the children feel their parent's break-up was their fault. They decide to carry the burden of guilt themselves. Be careful and look out for the child who appears to be harboring guilt and blame. Talk with the children and as I just mentioned, express your love and reassure them that they *are not to blame.* Look for the warning signs of guilt and burdens carried by a child.

•Sad expressions
•With drawn
•Stays away from other family members

•Comments like "I did it, it's my fault, I wish I were dead, I'm going to run away!"

There are cases where children will do and say things to obtain attention, but if you look carefully you will see the difference. Take time and observe.

COMPETITION

Another emotional landmine is competition and rivalry between children. Sibling rivalry, however, is only one of the many challenges facing the blended family. There will be competition for attention from parents, grandparents, friends, and ex-spouses. Each parent's birth children will also compete with the new spouse for attention. Learn to address and recognize when this type of challenge begins to take place. Sit down and discuss a plan of action with your spouse first, then conduct a family meeting with all parties involved.

I've stepped on some of these landmines in the early stages of our blended family. The most important thing to remember here is that if we fail to look for the hidden landmines, we may at some point unknowingly step on one that will explode right before our eyes, damaging the very foundation we are attempting to build.

Wear your body armor, be aware of the landmines that exist in your blended family and prepare yourself in the event one might explode. Learn the responses, actions and reactions of those in your blended family before it's too late. If one explodes, have your first-aid kit ready for immediate use. Do not let the wounds go untreated.

TIPS FOR REMARRIED PARENTS

Remarriage can be very stressful, especially in the blended family. The divorce rate is estimated at over 60% for second marriages. Why are there more divorces in second marriages than in first marriages? We would think that after one failed marriage, caution and consideration would be exercised before proceeding into another marriage, but apparently that is not the case.

Below are some tips for couples who have a blended family as a result of re-marriage.

• Give your spouse time to develop a relationship with your children.
• Listen to your spouse and what they observe with your children.
• Allow your spouse and their children to have a chance to interact and do things alone.
• Do things alone with your child occasionally and assure them with words and actions of your love for them.
• Be honest with your spouse, tell them how you feel.

The following letter was given to me by a friend who had it anonymously forwarded to her. Read the letter carefully and consider making it a part of the commitment to your spouse.

The spouse writes . . . .
"We belong together! You have shown me a kind of love I've never felt before and opened the door to a life I'd never anticipated. I know that sometimes you feel guilty for "burdening" me with so much baggage from your former life: the ex-spouse, the kids, and the child support! But it's a testament to my love for you that I chose to stand by you and face it all.

And I plan on continuing to stand by you to help you parent your children. Sometimes it's very hard for me, in ways you may not have imagined. I look at your children and I don't really know them. I can't really know them the way you do because they're part of you. That saddens me.

And sometimes I look at them and see your ex-spouse, a reminder that you haven't always been mine. That saddens me too. It's difficult for me to feel this kind of "separation" from a child in my care. I try to be as nurturing as I know how to be, but I don't know what to expect in return. It's confusing for me more often than not.

I know how much you love me, and how much you care about my feelings. I know you just want everyone in our family to be happy. **My relationship to Christ, you, and our marriage is my first priority, and we will address all issues together."**

What a powerful letter. Did you sense the commitment she had to her husband and the family? More importantly she tells us that with Christ first and her spouse and marriage second, they will survive.

THE RE-BREAKABLE BOARD:

A few years ago I studied a martial art called Tae Kwon Do. I had a fine Christian instructor who taught me many things. One of the first things I had to prepare for early into my study of Tae Kwon Do was board breaking, using my hands and feet. I was very intimated by this requirement.

Where would I get the power to perform such a difficult task? I made a decision to purchase a practice board, or re-breakable board as it is called.

The board is made of a heavy-duty material capable of supporting at least 250lbs of solid weight. The middle of the board has a circle painted on it. The circle is your target, or focal point used when performing a break. You must focus on the center of the mark in order to perform a "clean break," or damage to the hand and feet could occur very quickly.

There were times when I took my eyes off the center mark and hit outside the target area, causing severe bruising. On two occasions, I failed to place the board on a good solid support, which caused the board to slip, recoil and bounce back, hitting my hand and face unexpectedly.

I learned several valuable lessons from my failure to concentrate and hit the center of mark.

1. It takes only a second to make a mistake and miss the mark.

2. If you miss the mark, injury can occur damaging you for life.
3. Failure to focus and concentrate leads to unwise decisions.
4. Failure to have a good support structure, leaves you open for unexpected accidents.
5. Lack of concentration, getting in a hurry and lack of preparation, leads to mistakes.

As I began writing "Building a Building," I thought of the family in relationship to the things I just mentioned and how they relate to the Christian life. The mark of a Christian is one who seeks God and strives to walk in the light of Jesus Christ.

The same applies to each member of a family, regardless of its status. When we take our eyes off Christ and the things of God, we miss the mark and fall, we become spiritually injured. Keeping a blended family together requires focusing on the mark, the mark being Jesus Christ.

IS YOUR FAMILY COMMUNICATING?

A research and study conducted on the causes of heart disease revealed that individuals who are unable to communicate well are at a greater risk of high blood pressure, heart attack and cardiovascular disease.

James Lynch a well-known psychologist describes the concept of a "communication membrane" which exists between people in a family. The better able family members are at identifying and expressing their feelings, the more quickly their blood pressure returns to normal when emotional excitement occurs. However when we are unable to identify and verbally express our feelings, our physical and emotional well-being is in jeopardy.

I ask you, "Is it worth it?"

As a child I grew up in a family where there was no divorce, no violence, no drug or alcohol abuse, yet my family was dysfunctional. Why? Very simply, there was very little love and almost no communication shown and expressed towards one another. I was an only child and felt so alone in my own home.

All I wanted was for my dad to spend time with me. For years even after becoming an adult, I still wanted to spend quality time with my dad. I wanted to go fishing, go to the movies, stand in the yard and throw a football or baseball, go to the park, or just sit and ask my dad's advice on things. My father worked very hard to support our family and I understand that. However, had he only taken the time, if only for a few minutes a day just to talk with me, walk with me, throw a baseball to me, it would have been worth more than the world could ever offer.

Over the past several years my father and I have grown closer and now we are doing things together. Today my dad and I take walks; we talk and discuss things regarding our family, the news and society. I am getting to know my father and every minute with him is priceless.

The walks we take are slow ones now because he has aged and has a physical impairment. Regardless, it's never too late and I will cherish each and every moment as though I were a child again. What I am saying here is please take the time, if only for a moment, to talk, to listen to your children, your step children, your family. There may be a day you wish you had.

Poor communication skills can be passed down through generations if we grow up in families with parents and siblings who will not, or have not been instructed in the ways of effective communication. A child's self-esteem develops in relationship to the people who love and raise him.

To be loved, listened to, and understood is something we all desire and need in order to develop a solid understanding of ourselves in the world. If we enter into a blended family relationship with the inability to cope, communicate and relate, then the problems that arise as a result of everyday blended family life will increase. Reach out to your spouse, children and family. It is never too late.

Throughout our adult lives, our sense of self-worth is connected to our need and desire to communicate with others. The following is a prime example of what happens when words are not spoken and communication fails.

A rather crude and cruel experiment was carried out by Emperor Frederick, who ruled the Roman Empire in the thirteenth century. He wanted to know what man's original language was: Hebrew, Greek, or Latin? He decided to isolate a few infants from the sound of the human voice. He reasoned that they would eventually speak the natural tongue of man. Wet nurses who were sworn to absolute silence were obtained, and though it was difficult for them, they abided by the rule. The infants never heard a word—not one sound was uttered from the mouth of the nurses. Within several months all the infants died.

What does this tell us concerning the importance of communicating with children our family and others, especially new born children?

Effective communication within the blended family is a must, a basic emotional requirement and everyday necessity. If we fail to communicate properly and effectively, we close the door of understanding and open the doors of stress and misunderstanding.

Families become dysfunctional when they fail to communicate. This will lead to problems that are hard to solve. Communicating, praying, and paying close to the needs of your blended family are vital. Why? So often failure to communicate is key contributor to the break-up of a bended family.

Are there any communication problems in your family? If so record any area that requires attention.

_____

_____

_____

_____

_____

HOW TO MAKE A BLENDED FAMILY WORK:

When it comes to building, or re-building a blended family, here are some tips that will greatly enhance, reduce and even eliminate potential problems and stress for the parent and stepparent.

Provide neutral territory. If your budget allows, consider moving into a new home.

Don't try to be something you're not. Be yourself.

Set limits and enforce them. The parent and stepparent need to work out the rules of discipline in advance, and then support each other when the rules are being enforced.

Provide an outlet for children to use when it comes to dealing with and confronting their emotions regarding the stepparent, or the biological parent.

In most cases children will maintain affection for their natural parent, so step parents, please do not take it as a personal, or frontal attack when a step child treats you differently.

•Be patient and try to understand a stepchild's feelings. Feelings of love and hate by the stepchild may change every few hours, or few days.

•Avoid mealtime conflict. Some of greatest conflict can occur at the dinner table. Mealtime can bring back negative feelings caused by conflict at the dinner table from a previous family setting. Work smart at making times at the dinner table enjoyable and as peaceful as possible.

•Don't expect love and acceptance overnight.

•Don't take all the responsibility. The children have some, too. There are two people involved in any relationship. Therefore, if things are less than perfect, don't take all the guilt.

•Be patient. The first few months, or years, may not be easy.

•Maintain the privacy of the marital relationship. A solid

stepfamily relationship is based on a strong a marital bond between the husband and wife.

Building a blended family takes time and patience. Do not give up or in to the pressures of blended family life. Like any other family unit, it too can be healthy and strong.

Is a worry free life possible within a blended family?

Worry is one of the major causes of stress and heart disease among adults in our country today. Do you worry, and if so, why?

If you are a Christian and know Jesus Christ as your personal Savior, then you will understand the following scripture. Matthew chapter 6:25, Jesus says, *"So my counsel is: don't worry about things - food, drink, and clothes. For you already have life and a body - they are far more important than what to eat and wear."*

Below is a list of items pertaining to worry.

•Worry is unscriptural.

•Worrying is senseless. What does worrying achieve?

•Worrying is useless. It has no form or substance. It has no meaning and does not serve a purpose to life.

•Worrying is faithless. Can we be a Christian and have no faith?

•Worrying is Godless. If we believe in God then why worry.? Trust in him for all things and for all the answers.

•Worrying hinders family unity. It weakens the tie that binds us. To worry is to teardown the faith we have in each other and in God.

•Worrying is impracticable. It makes no sense. There is no practical reasoning behind the need to worry. Although it may seem natural, as professing Christians let us understand that worrying is contrary to God's word and destroys everything you and I profess to believe in.

1. Do you worry about things you have no control over? Have you given them to God?

2. List the things that create worry in your life.

_____

_____

_____

_____

_____

3. How will you eliminate the desire to worry from your thoughts?

_____

_____

_____

Chapter 6

The Biological Factor

Developing a blended family is a challenge unlike anything I've ever experienced before in my life. One of the biggest battles I fought in the early stages of building our new blended family was the **"Biological Factor"** as I call it. I adopted my wife's four sons, yet still had to deal with this issue from time to time, especially when it came to discipline.

Parental favoritism or the perception of parental favoritism can be and in most cases usually is a major problem for the blended family. This was the case for my wife and I. Of all the problems and attacks on our marriage, I would say it had to be the "blood issue" that created many of the battles we fought. If a parent is truly honest, the feelings for a biological child will conflict with the feeling you have for your stepchild. Do you agree or disagree?

God began a healing process in my life on this subject. Through God's word it was revealed to me that I must love equally in accordance with the way Christ loved His church, His people, and me. Christ loves us for whom and what we are; His love is not drawn according to bloodlines, or conditions.

I realized that children in blended family settings feel a sense of loss from the family setting they were once use to. Many children who may be dealing with emotions of this type need the freedom to mourn, yet need to feel and know that you are there for them when and if they need to discuss their feelings.

In so many cases, a newly married couples' biological children will experience emotions and feelings different from what they thought or even comprehended.

If you have entered into a blended family relationship, believing that you can treat yours and his or yours and hers without experiencing any problems or mixed emotions, think again and search your feelings.

Be prepared to experience some unexpected emotions and reactions as you work at parenting from "both sides of the coin." Don't rush into thinking or believing that feelings for a stepchild can be exactly the same as those you have for your biological child.

There are many cases where stepparents feel they can adjust and accept another individual's children thinking and believing there will be this "instant love connection" as I call it. Go slow, get to know your new or future spouse's children and take time to nurture your relationship with them before **ASSUMING** everything will be okay.

When the mother or father of biological children assume the responsibility as a step mother or step father, a whirlwind of unexpected emotions blow through, catching the parents off guard. In many cases the parents assume new full-time roles as both mom / step mom and as dad / step dad, for both sets of children.

So often biological children become jealous and exhibit resentment towards the way their mother treats her new step children or the manner in which the father treats his step children. Do you think new spouses in second marriages enter into blended family relationships with expectations that are too high? I did. It is imperative that parents teach their biological children the importance of connecting with their new family.

High expectations lead to miscommunication, false accusations, arguments, stress and tension between spouses and family. Over half of remarriages fail, in part because of the lack knowledge obtained regarding blended families. Assumptions, unrealistic expectation, and poor communication skills often contribute to the demise of couples who remarry and this often happens during the initial developmental stages of a newly formed blended family.

I cannot over emphasize the importance of assessing, counseling and talking with other blended families prior to entering into a new marriage / blended family relationship.

In new marriages involving blended families both spouses *must work together* through the times when and if difficulties arise to meet the challenge and develop strategies designed to refocus the family. In blended families the success of the relationship between the stepparent and stepchild is a key in keeping the family in harmony and securely connected.

No one said it would be easy. Step up to the plate, do the right thing and set the example for all to see. It is the God-given responsibility to develop an environment that works for everyone.

SALES REPS FOR GOD

As a blended family we are sales representatives for God. Many companies employ inside and outside sales representatives or sales reps as we shall call them. Sales reps can make or break a company. Bad advertising can destroy a company's reputation, even years of work can be destroyed in just months, or weeks. As Christians we are sales reps for God, including our blended families.

Christian's represent and work for the most powerful family in the world—the family of God. Our COO **(Chief Operating Officer)** is God the Father. As sales reps for God, we have an awesome responsibility to promote and represent the cause of Christ. We work for the most powerful CEO in the entire universe. He expects us to give our all to HIM.

There are many companies who are concerned about the

well-being of their employees and families. Many corporations who have individuals in upper management expect their administrative staff to have a good family life. If things are good at home, things will be good at work. What an excellent vision statement.

God expects us to be concerned for our family as well and place Him first in our homes. As with a company expecting their employees to have a good home life, our Heavenly father expects us to place Him first in our home through His Son Jesus Christ. How can we be good sales reps for Christ and market the Christian faith if we cannot operate and manage our own home?

The CEO and COO of the Christian home are the father and mother. God expects us to operate our home according to the guidelines and procedures set forth in His precious Word. We *will be* held accountable for the manner in which we govern our homes and raise our children. I don't want to be fired form the job, do you?

1. Are you operating your home the way God instructs you too?

O YES   O NO

If you answered no, write down the things you feel hinder your family from operating the way it should.

_____
_____
_____
_____
_____
_____

2. Develop an action plan for your family, describing ways to "get your house in order."

_____

_____

_____

_____

_____

_____

CHAPTER 7

Becoming a Successful Stepparent

Adjusting to new family relationships takes time. Although individuals fall in love and decide to marry, children of the parents may not desire the same. Parents need realistic expectations concerning a child's period of adjustment in a new family setting. It takes time and patience to adjust to changes in the family structure. Biological parents and stepparents must understand that all new family members need time to adjust to their new blended family.

Today with more than half of all marriages ending in divorce and the majority of divorced individuals remarrying, the number of blended families is growing.

Before a couple considers remarriage that involves becoming a stepparent, they should seek God, pray and talk together about their concerns and feelings. As a new stepparent, consideration to all the positive and negative sides of remarriage, including ex-spouses and any other baggage that could be attached, must be taken. Discuss and plan for issues such as who has authority over which kids and when, who watches the kids when spouses are away, and how can we make visitation arrangements work without conflict from former spouses? **Promote communication and agreement between one another, especially the children.**

A stepparent and stepchild relationship contains all the ingredients **(when mixed the wrong way)** of creating some of the most explosive and unexpected emotions one will ever experience. Talking, understanding, reasoning, and being open to suggestions and compromise are essential elements in surviving a blended family relationship.

Would you believe that there are times when parents and children go to battle attempting to win attention / affection of the other parent or vice versa? These feelings are very real and must be recognized, yet minimized. Develop a battle plan. Go on the offensive, instead of the defensive. A battle, of this type can easily turn into a full scale territorial war for attention.

Parents call in the reserves and stick to the battle plan. A situation like this can generate many emotional casualties. Pray, seek God for direction, Follow His battle plan, the Bible. This aspect of positive growth in the blended family promotes a healthy attitude towards one another and sets the tone for stability and unity within the blended family.

FAMILY MEETINGS

Family meetings are very important; they allow time for family members to "air out their grievances." Family meetings prevent power struggles so often found in a blended family and provide children with just the right tools for determining their role in the family.

As a husband and wife and as a mother and father, sit down with your children during a "family meeting" and discuss the thoughts felt by each family member. It may take some time for all the family members to open up. However don't quit, keep trying; the rewards are well worth the effort.

What happens when opposition occurs between children? Use the family meeting to assist in resolving any opposition. In our blended family, sibling rivalry was almost non-existent. If it did become an issue, I met with the children separately then together to discuss their emotions. To this day, our children get along better than most biological brothers and sisters do.

When disputes between siblings or stepsiblings occur,

find a quite location to talk or take a drive and allow the child(ren) to vent their frustrations. I found that taking kids out for a pizza, or ice cream does wonders. Amazing what food does for the blended family.

FAMILY TRADITIONS

Another area of concern in the blended family is disagreement on family traditions and holiday schedules. Traditions and holiday customs can create problems when one or both sets of children are unhappy with the loss of routine procedures. To help bridge the gap and eliminate potential problems, encourage the children to develop new routines and new traditions together. Use the family meeting process, and if possible, consider giving the children some space to work out their differences. **(Without parental interference.)**

There may be times when there is no perfect solution to issues surrounding prior family traditions, or developing new ones. It takes time and patience to find the balance and develop a process that works for everyone. Adjustments may be required; however, take joy in knowing that the work is well worth the effort and the end result will set the tone for good things to come.

At times children in blended families will resent, or look at non biological family members as intruders, no matter how hard the stepparent, or step siblings try to form a good relationship. The resentment often takes extreme forms. This could very easily get underneath a stepparent, or step sibling's "skin" creating the urge to respond with equal resentment and or hostility. The new relationship between the adults quickly becomes strained because it feels like a no-win situation. How do we correct this type of problem? The answer is prayer, patience, family meetings create new family traditions and . . . . **PERSERVERENCE!!.**

STEPMOTHERS

The life of a stepmother can be very complicated and stressful sometimes. Being a stepmother can be very rewarding, yet emotionally draining at times. No matter what, never give up; seek God for guidance and direction.

Below is a story of a stepmom and the trials she faced with her new stepson.

(Author and source unknown)

My stepson Billy is a wonderful child. He can be a very difficult child at times. Like all children, he jumps from wonderful to horrible with no predictable pattern or warning.

He is moody. He has a sense of fairness that extends to everyone around him. He roots for the underdog.

He is hyper kinetic and as clumsy as a newborn pup. He has big brown eyes that beg you for love and tell the whole world the state of his heart. He's more like me than the children I gave birth to. My evil stepmother membership card was revoked when I fell in love with him. It was impossible not to.

Nine years ago Billy's mother left not only her husband, but Billy as well, not because she'd found herself, but because she also knew she was a drug addict. She couldn't raise her son as well as his father could. For a long time Billy never knew when he would see her, although things are more regular now.

She's been through a lot and Billy witnessed most of it from the sidelines. He's 12 now and still fiercely loyal to her, I think, because he has seen her pain and like most sons he wants to protect his mother. He loves her just because she is "Mom" and that's enough for him. Sometimes I think maybe he is trying to make up for all the awful things that have happened in her life. I can't prove that, but Billy is the kind of kid who will give his 5-year-old brother the candy bar he's been saving for a week. I think he'd give his mom a whole lot more if he could.

I am the woman who knows his favorite foods, tends his wounded knees, and feelings, and I valiantly keep my mouth shut over his choice of wardrobe. I'm the one who helps with that ridiculously detailed school project, gives him "the talk" over that C-minus on his report card and wakes up the minute he has a nightmare. I am all the things a mother is to any child, save one; I am not first in his heart. That place is reserved for his mother.

Billy isn't as sure of my love as my other children. He hasn't lived with his "real" mother since he was a toddler, but he knows he loves her best. With that childish logic of his, he sometimes reasons that therefore I must love my "real" children best. It's not true, but it affects our relationship all the same. Sometimes we dance around each other like two porcupines, scared of our own razor-sharp emotions.

All mothers have foul moods from time to time. A reasonably good mother can be a total grump for a day and not scar her children for life; her children are sure of their place in her affections. A reasonably good stepmother doesn't have this luxury. A bad day for a stepmother can usher in a week of insecurity for a stepchild. Too many bad days and you're looking at a lifetime of therapy bills.

They say that love is the answer, but I'm not sure I know the question. The fact that I love Billy is a wonderful thing. Here is this child who didn't put me through labor and yet I love him. Billy loves me too, but it hasn't made things any easier. If we didn't love each other—if we only liked each other—we wouldn't be so insecure.

My bad moods wouldn't send him into a tailspin; his bad moods wouldn't awaken a gnawing guilt in me. If we only liked each other, we could go through our days without stepping on each other's feelings because our feelings wouldn't be as large. When you are a stepmother in love, you work twice as hard for half the reward.

When you are a stepchild, you want to make everyone happy and still be loyal to your "real" mom. Love complicates stepfamilies. When people think of stepmothers, they usually think in terms of the "sacrifice" it is to be one. I've had people, out of the blue, attempt to sympathize with me about how hard it must be to raise and love someone else's child.

People just seem to assume that I find it harder to love him than to love the children who are "mine." These people are right, but not for the reasons they think. It's easy loving the kid; what's hard is always playing second fiddle to the woman who gave birth to him.

The gifts he makes in school for Christmas, Valentine's Day and Mother's Day always come home with her name on them. I suppose I should be glad that he trusts me enough to tell me how he wishes he could live with her and his dad, but it hurts to hear it. Sometimes, and this is the worst, he'll take a happy memory that should belong to me—a shopping trip, a funny story—and give it to her. In his mind it's her and not me who was there for all the fun.

I'm so jealous of that woman I could scream. She doesn't deserve all that unconditional love. I do. Sometimes I think those evil stepmothers of popular myth knew something that I didn't. They were cold and aloof out of self-preservation. Then I think of what his "real" mother is missing. She didn't get to read the first story he wrote.

She didn't witness his first crush, the first time he beat a video game and every other firsts that has happened in his life—since she left to live somewhere else. I get to experience all that. I get to watch him grow up. I get to share his childhood with him. She may get the presents and a stray memory or two, but I get all the real stuff.

When I get jealous or my feelings get hurt, I'll try to keep that in mind. The headaches, heartaches, and feelings of insecurity are just the unlikely wrappings around a wonderful gift. I may not be the biological mother, but most of the time I'm smart enough to realize that that doesn't mean I don't count. Whenever I look into Billy's eyes while he snuggles next to me on the couch,

90

I know better. I may be playing second fiddle, but the music is beautiful.

TIPS FOR STEPMOTHERS

1. Accept your role of stepmother and don't try to become the mother.
2. Understand relationships take time to develop. Love for your stepchildren will not happen overnight if at all. Work on liking them first.
3. Look for the good in them and respect them and their privacy.
4. Don't get into the blame game. You are not responsible for every misbehavior of your stepchild.
5. Seek understanding instead of blame.
6. Make yourself available for your stepchildren.
7. Do some activities with them to build rapport.
8. Work as a team with your husband to build new house rules and traditions.
9. Take care of yourself.
10. Participate in your own activities and hobbies. The better you feel, the easier it is to accept and love others.

GUIDELINES FOR STEPFATHERS

Stepfathers can make a difference in the life, not only with his biological children, but his step children. There are many cases where a step father has the potential of making a profound impact on his step child, because the child's real father is removed from the picture. What an honor to be able to help mold the life of a child in a positive way. By following the guidelines below success as a step father can be achieved.

1. Promote a solid relationship between your step children and their biological father.

In most cases where there is an active biological father, don't expect him to fade away. He doesn't need too. He is in the picture and it is important for him to be there for his children. What happens so often in second (or third) marriages is that everyone in the household tries to forget the ex-spouse completely and without regard.

So often biological fathers' are perceived as "mean, or bad dads." That may be true in some cases, but more often than not most biological fathers are good men, good dads and need their children.

Your stepchildren need their dad, don't become jealous and make negative comments about your wife's ex-husband. If you try to ignore his existence, trying to keep his life and memories in a closet, or on a shelf, so to speak, rest assured that sooner or later, probably during a confrontation, an emotional landmine will explode and emotional injury, or conflict will occur. This type of emotional landmine that explodes usually causes conflict and could be used as weapons against you and your wife.

Be open and honest about your stepchild's father. If he is still trying to be involved with his kids, encourage him in that, remembering that he is their father, and that they are his children. Children need to be with their mothers and fathers; they need to be reconciled with them as well, thereby creating a feeling of peace about their relationship with them. You may grow to have a lasting and rewarding relationship with your stepchildren, but setting yourself up as the "new father" and asking them to accept you as a replacement to their real father is only asking for trouble and unnecessary problems. Be a man of God, set the tone for the family, yourself, your children, your step children and mature in growth and in the goodness of the things of God.

If your stepchildren's father has an active role in their lives, you will never truly be a father to your stepchildren, but you can be a mentor and an example to the children. You may and probably will face real life obstacles but remember; respect and trust will be gained as a result of doing the right thing. You don't have blood connections to your children, so there won't be the natural emotional attachment, but the pressure and expectations biological fathers face won't be there as well

2. Talk about discipline and us it wisely.

One of the greatest places of stress and frustration for a new stepfather is knowing how and to what extent you should be involved in the discipline of your step children. Here are two examples that illustrate right and wrong ways of handling the situation:

I know that being a stepfather can and is a complicated thing at times. The thought of not being in control of the home is tough. In many cases, the mother may be somewhat lax on discipline while the father / stepfather desires to change things like I did.

Being a good stepfather has to do with parenting. You and your wife must, work out forms of proper discipline together. Repeat together.

3. Schedule a date and time away from the kids as a couple.

When conducting family conferences and seminars, I always mention how important it is for the husband and wife to spend time alone together. This will strengthen and revitalize the marriage. Besides the benefits you will see as a couple, your stepchildren will take great comfort in your commitment to one another. Some of the children may have seen one marriage end, and even blame themselves for it.

Please make your marriage work, make your new family work and make it a shining star. Children will receive a positive outlook on life each day when they see and sense the love and commitment between their biological parent and step parent at home.

Dates and time alone serve as times of reassessment and planning as a team. In many cases wives are referees of sorts between fathers and their children, they are even more essential where stepfathers are concerned. Your wife is really the key person in the situation. She knows you well, and she knows her kids. She also knows the children's father, his influence, strengths, and weaknesses. This can be a time of learning in which you ask each other for help and advice regarding your role, strengths and weaknesses in the blended family. Learn and grow from these times alone together.

4. Be accepting.

It is very important in the early stages of blended family life that parents begin installing the ability to accept one another. By that, I mean taking the time and effort to accept all members of the new family. Yes it will take some time getting used to the change in status, but rest assured your efforts are well worth the cost.

There will be times when you feel like an outsider. That's why it's so important for you to take the initiative and show the children unconditional love and acceptance. Be flexible when it comes to how you act, or react, and be a good role model of someone who cheerfully adapts to the challenges and changes of blended family life. Ones desire to willingly accept another's personality and faults could be contagious and create a positive change in the family unit.

Sincere praise and a sense of being proud of your children, be it biological or step will encourage them to accept you more easily.

5. Don't insist on having your step children call you dad.

Here is another mistake I made in the early stages of our blended family. In a blended family marriage, your wife brought her children some new (and not entirely welcomed) obligations and commitments that they did not desire to make. Forcing them to accept you "right off the bat" will probably create resentment.

Try this, allow the children to define their own comfort

zones as they relate to you. Your desire for a quick and smooth transition is natural, but it will be best served by patience, as you earn the respect and love of your wife's children in their time, not yours.

A stepfather is a stepparent, not a replacement father, in most cases. The words mother and father are special words to the lives and hearts of many children. Stepparents are just that, stepparents, yet as a stepparent (as I mentioned earlier) you can still play a major role in the emotional development of the child.

Children need structure today more than ever before. If you are fair and consistent, your children won't resent you for it. Set up family rules for the home as soon as possible so you spend less time disciplining and more time bonding. Children need parents, even visiting parents to set up predictable structures and limits.

In a home with structure, parents and children spend less time negotiating and arguing. Parent/child power struggles over repetitive issues waste time and undermine the child's self-esteem. Talk about real issues, create intimacy, communicate and discuss concerns with reachable goals.

Stepfathers can be guides, mentors, and even psychological fathers to stepchildrens over time. Go slow and take time, because you may very well be the only father figure your stepchildren will ever see.

Stepfathers, stepdads, pray, read God's Word, trust Him, seek God in all things, and live the example of Christ before your family. It is what God expects us to do; it is what we must do!

TEN STEPS TOWARD SUCCESSFUL STEPPARENTING

1. Provide neutral territory. If your budget allows, consider moving into a new home.
2. Don't try to fit a preconceived role. Be yourself.

3. Set limits and enforce them. The parent and stepparent need to work out disciplinary actions in advance, then support each other when the rules are being enforced.
4. Allow an outlet for children's feelings about the natural parent. The children will maintain affection for their natural parent. Do not take this personally.
5. Expect ambivalence. Feelings of love and hate by the stepchild may change every few hours, or few days. Avoid mealtime misery. Mealtime can be laden with emotions of "how it used to be." Try to make this time as peaceful as possible.
6. Don't expect instant love.
7. Don't take all the responsibility. The children have some, too. There are two people involved in any relationship. Therefore, if things are less than perfect, don't take all the guilt.
8. Be patient. The first few months, or years, may have difficult periods.
9. Maintain the privacy of the marital relationship. A solid stepfamily relationship is based on a strong marital relationship. Blending a family takes time and patience.
10. Like any other family unit, however, it too can be healthy and strong.

Source: Excerpted from "Ten Steps Toward Successful Stepparenting," by Karen S. Bruns, Ohio State University. For entire text refer to the following Internet address: **htt://www.ag.ohio-state.edu/~ohioline/hygfact/5000/5231.html**

GUIDELINES FOR STEPPARENTS

I found the following information and guidelines from various resources instrumental in building our blended family.

It is very helpful if a blended family start out in neutral territory like moving into their own house or apartment. Avoid moving into one of the spouse's homes if it was the biological family's home first.

As mentioned earlier, develop the habit of having a weekly family meeting. Allow each member of the family to speak freely on issues. Use the family meetings to plan vacations and fun. Accept influence from the children and give them a feeling of control by allowing them some say so in family decisions.

A healthy couple relationship is a must for a blended family to exist. The couple's relationship should come first with the children a very close second. A strong adult relationship can protect the children from another family loss, and it can provide the children with a positive model of what a good marriage looks like.

As a stepparent don't try to compete with the biological parent. Instead work on creating a friendship built on respect with your stepchildren. Let the biological parent do most of the discipline until the stepchild feels comfortable with your parental role.

If your family includes "visiting" children, understand that they usually feel strange and like outsiders in your neighborhood. It helps if they can have their own spaces in your home. This can be a drawer or shelf for their personal possessions that no one else has. Some place or space that is all a child's own is very helpful.

Include the "visiting" stepchildren in family chores and projects. They will feel more connected to the group in this way. Allow them to bring a friend with them occasionally to visit to help with the adjustment.

Because stepfamilies are born of loss, a mixture of feelings can show themselves quite often. These feelings include jealousy, rejection, guilt, anger, frustration, hurt and disappointment. Seek understanding when these feelings arise.

Allow them to surface and release. Empathize as much as possible. Try to walk in their shoes and feel their feelings.

LOYALTIES

Children have loyalties to parents. A child may feel that showing affection toward a stepparent is betraying the biological parent. The child who has lived in a single-parent household may have difficulty sharing that parent. Understand where they come from, Be patient.

Adults may also experience loyalty conflicts. Parents may feel guilty over not living with biological children. The stepparent may have difficulty accepting live-in stepchildren.

The new stepfamily creates new relationships. Family members may be unclear as to what their roles and expectations are within the family. Are the stepparents comfortable disciplining the children and enforcing the limits? Do the children know what role the new family members play? Do they know that their stepfather can assign chores to be done? How should they refer to the stepparent's parents?

GRANDPARENTS/STEP-GRANDPARENTS

Grandparents are also affected by new blended family relationships.

I want to take some time and address the role of grandparents in a blended family. Grandparents are a very important part of a new blended family. Blended families are developed as a result of the death or divorce in a nuclear family. Grandparents need to mourn the loss of that relationship before they can become a part of the stepfamily. Anger, resentment and fears are normal. Be patient, pray, seek God for direction and help.

Realize your value and what you have to offer as a step-grandparent.

Grandparents and stepparents are wonderful resourceful people. You have a lot to offer, such as unconditional love, family history, your life experience, and let's not forget WISDOM!

"It's hard to love them as my own grandchildren," were the words I heard many times from my mother. Why is it so hard? This was the question I asked my parents and myself. As we studied earlier, the biological factor is one of the many challenges faced by parents in a blended family. I never dreamed it would apply to grandparents. Why was it so hard for my parents to accept my adopted children as their grandchildren?

I prayed and searched God's Word for the answers. Here is what I found.

The Bible tells us to love one another and love our neighbor as ourselves. If so, then why is it so hard for grandparents who have biological grandchildren to love and accept adopted, or step grandchildren? The answer I believe lies in the heart. If we have the love of Christ in us, then the biological factor should never be an issue.

If it becomes an issue with one of your parents as it did mine, pray, seek God for guidance, be understanding and in love, schedule a time to meet with your parent(s) to discuss the issue.

There are no ex-grandparents, only ex-spouses.

Go slow and see where your grand parenting skills are needed. Be prepared for the emotions and conflicts associated with the blended family.

HOLIDAYS, TRADITIONS AND RITUALS

Maintain family rituals in your home, develop new ones that fit your new blended family and adapt to new traditions in the blended family.

Be an impartial sounding board to your grandchildren or step grandchildren. Listen to all your grandchildren, biological and bonus. At times they might need someone to talk to or just listen; they need you.

CHAPTER 8

Forgiveness:
A place of sanctuary for the blended family

PART 1

Now we come to one of the most important aspects of building a blended family. It may be the most important part in relationship to the success or failure of a blended family. Because of this, I have devoted two chapters to the subject. Without forgiveness you will not succeed as a blended family.

Forgiveness; the one word that will help build, re-build, heal and strengthen a blended family more than any other word in our language, or the world. Forgiving and putting forgiveness into action is the key process for emotional healing. As we look into the meaning of forgiveness, let me begin by saying, that when we allow forgiveness to operate in our lives and work in our hearts, positive changes will occur, not only affecting ourselves, but our family and those around us.

Forgiving others of their shortcomings allows for the development of trust which is so vital to the formation of a blended family. If family members believe and know they will be forgiven for their mistakes, or short comings, a sense of security is formed.

Forgiveness is a key element in building a strong foundation for the blended family. It provides strong structural support for the building of the family and is crucial when the storms of life begin to rage. Forgiveness lessens the load of guilt, shame, and bitterness, which so often enters in during the early stages of a new blended family. Forgiveness reduces the emotional load that could be carried into new family relationships. It also reduces potential conflict that might arise when a new blended family is under construction. *Forgiveness is a place of sanctuary for the blended family.*

Forgiveness promotes an atmosphere of unity and harmony and allows for increased opportunities of success. Not only is forgiveness a very powerful word, it is an act that helps blended families grow stronger together. As human beings we all fall and fail. We all need forgiveness at various points in our lives. Forgiveness is not for a selected few, it is for everyone.

What does the Bible say about forgiveness?

Jesus said in Mark 11:24–25
[24] Listen to me! You can pray for anything, and if you believe, you will have it.

[25] But when you are praying, first forgive anyone you are holding a grudge against, so that your Father in heaven will forgive your sins, too." *Holy Bible, New Living Translation,* (Wheaton, IL: Tyndale House Publishers, Inc.) 1996

What do we have to do to make forgiveness a way of life in the blended family? The following points will assist in the development of a forgiving attitude within the blended family.

Forgiveness, a Never Ending Process
For many, forgiveness can occur instantly. For others it takes time and patience. It is a continual process of canceling the debts of those who harm us, come against us and fail us. In Luke chapter 17: verses 3–4 we read that when our brother sins against us and repents we are to forgive him. We also read that

if he sins seven times a day and comes to us for forgiveness we forgive him. Let me add to that by saying even if someone does not come to us who has wronged us, sinned against us, we still need to forgive them, we must forgive them. Why? Harboring un-forgiveness is spiritual cancer. IT WILL DESTROY US IF LEFT UNTREATED.

Some might assume that what is important about the verses in Luke is that Jesus makes seven the greatest number of times we should have to forgive in a day. Jesus was teaching a principle of unlimited forgiveness. When Peter on another occasion asked, "'Lord, how often shall my brother sin against me, and I forgive him? Up to seven times?'

Jesus said to him, 'I do not say to you, up to seven times, but up to seventy times seven'" (Matthew 18:21–22). The process is unending.

Be careful when you ask forgiveness. The problem is not so much in the words themselves but in the motives of the person doing the asking. Many requests for forgiveness are nothing more than thinly veiled demands to avoid the pain of wrongs and harm done.

The truth often comes out if forgiveness is temporarily denied. If the offender tries to turn the tables and shame the hurt person into letting him off the hook, then it's apparent that the request for forgiveness is not an honest request. True repentance claims no rights while asking mercy for wrongs done. Real repentance expresses a broken, undemanding heart and a heart full of mercy.

In anticipation of future hurts, begin developing a heart of forgiveness and mercy.

The immediate pleasure of sweet revenge is only temporary. In the Sermon on the Mount, Jesus taught us to hunger for that which in time will prove more satisfying. He said, "Blessed are those who hunger and thirst after righteousness, for they will be filled," (Matthew 5:6). Here He approved of hungering for the ways of God who, in His time, will satisfy the longings of those who entrust their well being to Him.

Some of the "rightness" that can be hungered for includes a Christ like love for those who are presently harming us (Matthew 5:39–42; Luke 6:32–36). Such kindness might look mindless and even self-destructive to those who are living by the rules of this world. But this is the love that can distinguish us as followers of Christ and as grateful subjects of the kingdom of heaven.

Forgiveness is by far the most powerful process known to man, for removing bitterness, anger, hatred, etc. Forgiving someone can replace years of mental anguish, agony, and even poor health with a lifetime of peace and contentment. This might sound simple, yet for many it the most difficult task to perform. Let's look at why it is so hard for many of us to forgive.

UNFORGIVENESS

Before we can forgive, we must first break up the old foundation of unforgiveness. What does the foundation consist of? The old foundation is composed of various emotional ingredients, the main ingredients being bitterness and anger.

Bitterness comes from the word bitter, which Webster defines as **1. sharp to the taste, sorrowful, painful, resentful, etc.**

The definition provides a perfect description of how we feel when a person or group of people comes against us. Did you know bitterness cast the mold for a hardened heart? It can form our personality for years to come and shape our attitude towards friends, family and loved ones.

Over the years, I've had the opportunity to meet and counsel many people concerning unforgiveness. I found that in a vast majority of cases, the individuals themselves were raised in an environment where their parents harbored unforgiveness and anger. It is amazing how growing up in such a counter productive atmosphere of hidden unforgiveness and resentment affects a child's life throughout adulthood.

Bitterness and anger doesn't always have to be seen in a person, sometimes you can sense it, even feel it.

When you fail to deal with emotions such as unforgiveness, bitterness, anger, hatred, etc, you fail to love the way you should and you forge the chains that **will** bind you for a lifetime. *It's one thing for us to go through a bitter experience, yet another if we allow that experience to change us into a bitter and unforgiving person.*

The first lines of James 4:7 tells us to, **"Therefore submit to God. Resist the devil and he will flee from you."** Submitting to God **completely** gives us the power to forgive and resist any temptation brought about by our past.

Fear of failure is a common emotion we experience when bitterness from the past, a failed marriage, relationship, or loss mixes with anger and resentment towards a person, persons, or event creating our unforgiveness.

Although we face fear and uncertainty, although we become burdened with the struggles and trials of life, there is hope in serving God through Christ. The prophet Isaiah wrote and gives us encouragement on how to deal with the trials of life and where to find our strength.

In Isaiah chapter 41 verse 10 we read . . . . . .

[10]Fear not, for I am with you; Be not dismayed, for I am your God. I will strengthen you, Yes, I will help you, I will uphold you with My righteous right hand.' *The New King James Version,* (Nashville, TN: Thomas Nelson Publishers) 1998, c1982

When we've been hurt, or betrayed by actions, or words of those who say they love us, we turn on the motor of unforgiveness and based on the amount of pain, anger, and bitterness inside, many of us produce a lot of horse power to drive the unforgiving vehicle. When we look at problems and challenges through the eyes of bitterness, we see only clouds of negativity and will never be happy, no matter what this world has to offer.

When we look through the eyes of bitterness, the light that shines on our road to building a blended family becomes dim and we lose our way, but when we look through the eyes of forgiveness and seek God for help and understanding, the bitterness is replaced with a new light that shines even brighter.

Take a moment and answer the following questions.

1. What is your definition of unforgiveness?

_____

_____

_____

_____

_____

_____

2. What is your definition of forgiveness?

_____

_____

_____

_____

_____

3. Are you experiencing any form(s) of unforgiveness bitterness in your life now?

O YES   O NO

If so, list the things, or individuals you feel are creating the bitterness.

_____

_____

_____

Once we've identified the source(s) of our bitterness/ unforgiveness, the next step is to begin building a new foundation in our hearts consisting of **forgiveness, love, compassion and understanding,** so we can proceed to the next step, which is to forgive and move forward in our healing.

How do we do this? First let's look at the definition of forgiveness. Webster defines forgiveness as: **1. giving up wanting to punish, 2. pardon, 3. forgiving.** Read the definition again. Isn't that powerful? The ability to forgive is an act of kindness, love and compassion. It allows us to remove the past from our memory to where it no longer affects our physical and emotional well being.

Although it may take time to completely forget the things that initiated bitterness, anger, or un-forgiveness, we **must** forgive in order for God to begin a work in us. I can say from first hand experience that in divorce, there is no person, group of people, place, or thing worth emotionally dying for. Trust God, pray, forgive and work on forgetting the past, moving forward, leaving it behind

When unforgiveness exists in our lives, it robs us of our emotional and spiritual lively hood. Unforgiveness is a breeding ground for anger, unhappiness, hatred, etc. and affects our health, our friends, families and job. We can lose all that is precious to us.

Forgiveness is not a feeling, it is something that we must do, need to do and as Christians, God expects us to do. Although forgiveness is a choice, it is the right choice, because it leads to happiness, contentment and moving forward. There will be times when people refuse to accept, or acknowledge our forgiveness. There will be times when individuals refuse to forgive us of our errors and mistakes.

Whatever the case may be, if we ask God to forgive us and we in turn ask for or give forgiveness, then our account has been settled and we are debt free.

Bitterness = emotional and spiritual death
Forgiveness = happiness and new life!

True forgiveness comes from God through Jesus Christ; true happiness comes from serving God and seeking to do His will. Let's look at forgiveness according to God's Word and His plan.

In order for us to forgive unconditionally, we must be forgiven. All we have to do is simply ask Jesus Christ into our hearts and lives, ask Him to forgive us of our sins and believe upon Him. Putting off forgiveness only prolongs the hurt and bitterness, causing wounds and scars when left untreated, to become infected.

In order to properly manage a blended family, we must have the ability to forgive and accept forgiveness. Exercising forgiveness in the home is an expression of love towards our spouses and children. In order to forgive and be forgiven, we must have a submissive heart towards God. It's not always an easy task to submit to God completely; it takes time, dedication, prayer, fasting and reading God's Word, but the reward is great and far reaching.

Let's look at what God's word has to say concerning forgiveness.

Isaiah 44:22

[22] I have swept away your sins like the morning mists. I have scattered your offenses like the clouds. Oh, return to me, for I have paid the price to set you free." *Holy Bible, New Living Translation,* (Wheaton, IL: Tyndale House Publishers, Inc.) 1996.

Matthew 6:14–15

[14] "If you forgive those who sin against you, your heavenly Father will forgive you. [15] But if you refuse to forgive others, your Father will not forgive your sins. *Holy Bible, New Liv-*

ing Translation, (Wheaton, IL: Tyndale House Publishers, Inc.) 1996.

Matthew 18:21 and 22

[21] Then Peter came to him and asked, "Lord, how often should I forgive someone who sins against me? Seven times?" [22] "No!" Jesus replied, "seventy times seven!

Mark 11:25

[25] But when you are praying, first forgive anyone you are holding a grudge against, so that your Father in heaven will forgive your sins, too." *Holy Bible, New Living Translation,* (Wheaton, IL: Tyndale House Publishers, Inc.) 1996.

Luke 6: 37

[37] "Stop judging others, and you will not be judged. Stop criticizing others, or it will all come back on you. If you forgive others, you will be forgiven. *Holy Bible, New Living Translation,* (Wheaton, IL: Tyndale House Publishers, Inc.) 1996.

Ephesians 4:31 and 32

[31] Get rid of all bitterness, rage, anger, harsh words, and slander, as well as all types of malicious behavior. [32] Instead, be kind to each other, tenderhearted, forgiving one another, just as God through Christ has forgiven you. *Holy Bible, New Living Translation,* (Wheaton, IL: Tyndale House Publishers, Inc.) 1996

Ephesians 5:1 and 2

Follow God's example in everything you do, because you are his dear children. [2] Live a life filled with love for others, following the example of Christ, who loved you and gave himself as a sacrifice to take away your sins *Holy Bible, New Living Translation,* (Wheaton, IL: Tyndale House Publishers, Inc.) 1996

Throughout the Bible, we're told of how forgiveness gives joy, peace, and eternal life.

All we have to do is ask. Receiving forgiveness from God comes simply by asking with a sincere heart and desire. The greatest gift is free. When we ask Jesus into our heart and life, then the chains of bondage are removed and we are free to forgive without reservation, or condition.

The unbeliever will rationalize forgiveness; the unbeliever may not accept it and in most cases will not ask for it because he knows not the love and forgiveness found through Jesus Christ. The born again Christian serving Christ knows and understands the meaning of forgiveness, for they have experienced true forgiveness by faith in Christ, the Cross, and believing upon His name. Asking for forgiveness and being able to forgive will open the doors to peace, happiness and a stress free life.

Here is an example of how God performed a miracle in my life when I chose to ask forgiveness for something I failed to do. For months I battled the calling of God in my life. I wondered why and kept searching for the answers. I finally realized that there were certain things in my past I needed to make right and although forgiven by God, I needed to personally address these issues the way a Christian man should, especially this one particular issue.

Here is the account of what happened:

After my divorce in 1994, I owed money to the attorney who handled my divorce. I was upset over the amount of money charged for his services. Bitterness and anger set in and I paid him very little towards the amount owed. It soon got to the point where I stopped paying and discarded all the bills sent to me. Although my attorney did nothing wrong, I used him as an outlet and an excuse for the pain I was experiencing as a result of my divorce.

Several years passed, then one day after finally realizing I needed to stop running from God, ask Him to forgive me, and do His will, the Lord spoke to me in this still small voice. He let me know that before I could move forward and do the work he had for me, I needed to take inventory and personally undo any wrong I had committed.

The one thing that kept coming to mind was the debt I owed the attorney who handled my divorce case. I couldn't wait anymore; I had to do the right thing. I called his office and made an appointment to see him. On the morning of my appointment I arrived at his office 30 minutes early. I sat in my car praying and reading my Bible. I asked God to go before me and prepare me for whatever I would face.

I began walking along side the building towards the entrance wondering what was about to happen. What do I say? What do I do? God help me. As I began my climb up the two flights of stairs leading to the attorney's office, I could feel my heart become heavy and my spirit began to break. I knew I was on the verge of breaking down in tears. I went into the office, walked to the receptionist desk and introduced myself. I began to explain why I was there, not knowing what was about to happen.

The receptionist told me to have a seat, and a few minutes later she came back to inform me that the attorney had to go to a funeral and could not see me. I was heart-broken because I wanted to personally ask him for my forgiveness. She said I'm sorry, but can I help you. I stood up, followed her back to her desk and began to explain my reason for the appointment. I began to speak; just a few words came out of my mouth. Then all of a sudden I began to weep, telling this lady **(whom I'd never met)** that I was there to ask for forgiveness for not paying a debt I owed.

As tears streamed down my face, I explained to this woman (a total stranger) that when God does a work in your life you have to make things right before you can move on and do the work God has planned for you. I told her I had only $500.00 to pay towards the amount due. I knew I owed thousands of dollars. **($6,000.00 to be exact.)**

She didn't know this, but I had the title to my car in my left coat pocket ready to use for paying off the remaining balance. As she was making a phone call to locate my attorney, I asked for a piece of paper to write a letter of forgiveness.

I finished writing, stood up, walked to her desk, handed the letter to her for the attorney, and asked her to please tell him I was sorry and to forgive me. Once again I told her I didn't know how I would pay the balance. I started to offer her the title to my car as payment for the remaining balance, but before I could, she stood up, looked at me with a smile and softly spoke these words, **"Don't worry about it, your debt has been paid."**

I looked at her and said excuse me? She spoke saying, **"Your account is settled; it's paid in full."** Can you imagine what went through my mind? While I was writing the letter of forgiveness to the attorney, she called him to let him know I was there. During their conversation, he instructed her to mark my debt paid in full. As I walked out of the office, I was reminded of a song entitled "Paid in Full." You see Christ died on the cross for our sins. **He paid our sin debt in full.**

Is there is anyone you know who needs forgiving (especially your family)? Do you need to ask for forgiveness? Do it today without hesitation, so you can experience the full blessings of God. Colossian chapter three verses twelve through fourteen give us instruction and direction on how to live in harmony and a life free of bitterness, anger, resentfulness, and hatred.

Colossians: 3: 12–14

[12] Since God chose you to be the holy people whom he loves, you must clothe yourselves with tenderhearted mercy, kindness, humility, gentleness, and patience.

[13] You must make allowance for each other's faults and forgive the person who offends you. Remember, the Lord forgave you, so you must forgive others.

[14] And the most important piece of clothing you must wear is love. Love is what binds us all together in perfect harmony.

New Living Translation, (Wheaton, IL: Tyndale House Publishers, Inc. 1996)

Take a moment and answer the following questions
1. Why do I need to forgive my spouse, children, friends, family, etc?

_____

_____

_____

_____

_____

_____

2. What are the benefits of forgiveness?

_____

_____

_____

_____

_____

When we seek forgiveness and ask Jesus Christ into our lives, we receive a reward that will last throughout all eternity. As time goes on and as we journey through life, we'll be required to forgive again and again and again. The circumstances may not be as horrific, or trying as what we face now, but the results of being able to truly forgive will be the same.

Question: How do we know there is forgiveness from God?

Answer: **John 3:16–18**

[16]"For God so loved the world that he gave his only Son, so that everyone who believes in him will not perish but have eternal life. [17]God did not send his Son into the world to condemn it, but to save it. [18]"There is no judgment awaiting those who trust him. But those who do not trust him have already been

judged for not believing in the only Son of God. *Holy Bible, New Living Translation,* (Wheaton, IL: Tyndale House Publishers, Inc.) 1996

1. If we ask for forgiveness then what will happen?

_____

_____

_____

_____

_____

_____

2. What is the one thing we must do in order to receive forgiveness from God?

_____

_____

_____

_____

_____

_____

3. When we ask for forgiveness, what does God do? Isaiah 43:25

_____

_____

_____

_____

_____

_____

4. What does Matthew 5:44 tell us concerning praying?

_____

_____

_____

_____

_____

5. What does Proverbs 16:7 say to you on how to live at peace and in harmony with those who come against us?

_____

_____

_____

_____

_____

_____

6. Is the ability to forgive those who have come against us a one time act or procedure?

_____

_____

_____

_____

_____

_____

7. How should I react if the other person/spouse, my ex, does not respond?

_____

_____

_____

_____

_____

_____

8. How do I keep unforgiveness from resurfacing?

_____

_____

_____

_____

_____

_____

9. How can I truly know that I have been forgiven?

_____

_____

_____

_____

_____

_____

10. What does forgiveness bring?

_____

_____

_____

_____

_____

FORGIVING AND LEARNING TO FORGIVE

One of the major aspects of healing is the ability to forgive and ask for forgiveness.

Consider the following questions.
1. Why is it so important to forgive?
2. Should we forgive?
3. What happens if we do not forgive?
4. What are the results of unforgiveness?
5. Can God forgive us if we cannot forgive?

FORGIVENESS CONSISTS OF

- Deciding to accept what has happened and truly forgive.
- Forgiving and not returning to the past.
- Trusting and obeying God for forgiveness.

We must:
- Live above our circumstances, trials and problems.

- Take responsibility for our actions, feelings, and attitudes **(If necessary, "clean the slate").**
- Never expect or require a response from people we forgive.

Did you know there are victims of unforgiveness? Do you know who the real victims are? Many people think that by not forgiving they "get back" at those who have hurt them, but in reality the real victim is the one who cannot forgive. The longer we wait to forgive, the longer it takes to heal. We have a free will. We can accept Christ or reject Him. We can forgive or harbor unforgiveness; the choice is ours. Bitterness, anger, hatred and resentfulness, are the ingredients of unforgiveness.

Scripture verses:

Matthew 18; 23–27
Instruction and a Parable Concerning Forgiveness:
[23] Therefore the kingdom of heaven is like a certain king who wanted to settle accounts with his servants. [24] And when he had begun to settle accounts, one was brought to him who owed him ten thousand talents. [25] But as he was not able to pay, his master commanded that he be sold, with his wife and children and all that he had, and that payment be made. [26] The servant therefore fell down before him, saying, 'Master, have patience with me, and I will pay you all.' [27] Then the master of that servant was moved with compassion, released him, and forgave him the debt. *The New King James Version,* (Nashville, TN: Thomas Nelson Publishers) 1998, c1982

CHAPTER 9

Forgiveness

PART 2

FORGIVING OTHERS

Ephesians 4:32 [32] And be kind to one another, tender-hearted, forgiving one another, even as God in Christ forgave you.

As I mentioned earlier, one of the biggest obstacles in the family today is the inability to forgive. Some hearts are harder than others; some grow hard over the years.

Everyday we are bombarded with news of tragedies, violent acts, and suffering people. Living sanely in such a world often necessitates developing a certain amount of thick skin. Unfortunately, a thick skin and a hard heart are often confused with one another. Instead of developing a thick skin, many develop a hard heart, and as a result, you can find hard people everywhere in our society. Unfortunately, their hardness has made them cynical and unforgiving.

Do you find it difficult to follow the command you just read in Ephesians 4:32? Consider the following:

A teenager, tired of reading bedtime stories to his little

sister, decided to record several of her favorite stories on tape. He told her, "Now you can hear your stories anytime you want. Isn't that great?" She looked at the machine for a moment and then replied, "No. It hasn't got a lap." The truth is, we all need a lap and tender loving relationships with those we love.

Each and every one of us need tender loving relationships. We all need to know we are loved, accepted and forgiven. Sadly, while we need love, acceptance and forgiveness, often we find it hard to forgive. We find it hard because our hearts have become hard.

The message of Ephesians 4:32 is really directed to those of us who want to be able to forgive but maybe we've allowed our hearts to become hardened. So often we become the Harry and Hazel hard-hearts, perhaps a little overly tough in our approach. We've lost the balance. There are times you need to have a thick skin. But you can become hard hearted instead and can do serious damage, both to others and to yourself as well.

If we are honest with ourselves, we have to admit that sometimes other people really get under our skin. We don't want them to, but it seems we are unable to do anything about it. They aggravate us, offend us, and we become hard towards them. We know we should not feel this way, but we do. We should forgive and forget, but can't—period, end of statement so to speak. Why? The answer is that our hearts have been placed in an ice chest and are cold. Forgiveness freezes the heart to the point it doesn't generate any warmth. As Christians we must be warm, tenderhearted, forgiving and loving towards one another, even those who come against us.

At our rare times of introspection, we do desire to be more tenderhearted and forgiving, but we seem to have unlearned those emotions. How can we regain and rekindle the fire of forgiveness? What are some practical steps we can take to develop a little more tenderness? How can we develop a forgiving spirit? How can we be, as the Scripture exhorts us, more tenderhearted, kind, and forgiving?

LOVING AS CHRIST LOVES

What we are talking about here is loving the way Christ loved us, seeing as God sees others, feeling as others feel, and then doing something about it. That is what Christ did for us. That is what we should and must do for others.

The Bible tells us to *"Be kind to one another, tenderhearted, forgiving one another, as God in Christ forgave you."*

God has always had time for us. He has always listened to us. His forgiveness was made possible because of His love for the world.

When we learn to forgive, we then learn to love as Christ loves us. As Christians we need to slow down and express our genuine love and affection for each other.

What would happen if we were able to do this? I believe that the results would be extraordinary. People would be wondering what happened to old Harry and Hazel Hard-heart. Our spouses and children would be overjoyed. The superficial relationships we have would deepen. Our churches would be filled as people would discover that church is a place where they can find love, forgiveness, and genuine acceptance.

Many people are afraid to forgive. I like what C.S. Lewis said when he addressed fear in forgiving. He said, "To love at all is to be vulnerable. Love anything, and your heart will be certainly wrung and possibly be broken. If you want to make sure of keeping it intact, you must give your heart to no one, not even to an animal. Wrap it carefully round with hobbies and little luxuries; avoid all entanglements; lock it up safe in the casket or coffin of your selfishness. But in that casket—safe, dark, motionless, airless—it will change. It will not be broken; it will become unbreakable, impenetrable, and irredeemable."

Yes, there could be danger in loving, but there is a greater danger in not loving. The danger is that your heart grows hard and unforgiving. You become bitter and hardhearted. If you want to be able to break the shell of hardness, which grows around your heart, choose to love others. If you do not, you will never be able to forgive others.

The challenge now lies before us. Let us learn to see others as God sees them, valuable, important, and special. Learn to feel as others feel—to walk a mile in their shoes and to consider what it would be like to be in their situation.

Finally and most importantly, learn to love and forgive others as Christ loves and forgives us. By expressing love and compassion towards our family members, including others who come against us, we are able to forgive and live a free and joyous life.

Forgiveness transforms our home into a place alive with the power of God and the love of Christ working in the hearts of each and every family member.

Questions to Consider:
Have you been forgiven by someone in your past?

How did it make you feel?

Are you able to freely forgive others?

1. In what ways has the daily grind of living in the world harden your heart?

_____

_____

_____

_____

_____

_____

2. What effect does unforgiveness have in relationship to building a blended family?

_____

_____

_____

_____

_____

_____

3. How do we soften our hearts and become more understanding and forgiving?

_____

_____

_____

_____

_____

_____

DEVELOPING AN ACTION PLAN

Developing an action plan, or battle plan as I call it, is a powerful process for dealing with the emotions brought about by a hurtful act, be it intentional, or unintentional. The sole purpose of the action plan is to format and develop a strategy for combating any unforgiveness, or bitterness in your life.

STEPS TO CONSIDER BEFORE DEVELOPING AN ACTION PLAN:

Think about the circumstances and events surrounding your feelings of unforgiveness, bitterness, anger, etc. Carefully consider and meditate on the following questions:
•What really happened? **(Did I contribute to any of this?)**

- Could the situation creating my bitterness have been prevented?
- How did I react? **(Did my reactions further complicate the problem?)**
- Did I over react to the situation? **(Am I too sensitive? Do I get my feelings hurt to easily?)**
- Who are the perpetrators?
- Is it worth dying emotionally and physically over something I have no control over?
- Who is affected by my unforgiveness?

EMOTIONS AND SIGNS OF UNFORGIVENESS

Unforgiveness, the emotions and stress associated with everyday life, tend to go unnoticed and often hinder family development. These signs and symptoms come in many forms and over time have the potential of creating serious problems for the family. In some cases, we withdraw from our spouses, families, and friends.

When we fail to forgive and address the specific emotions that plague our families. Stagnation sets in, prolonging our resolve.

Well-known authors, professors, ministers, and other individuals who write books and material on the subject of human emotions have experienced the same as you and me.

It grieves my spirit when people try to scientifically rationalize and explain our God-given emotions by promoting ways of healing that are detrimental to our spiritual, mental, and physical well-being. **True healing comes from God though Christ.**

Below is a list of emotions commonly found when husbands, wives, mothers, fathers brothers, sisters, step brothers, step sisters and others attempt to forgive, yet are unable too because of the walls constructed by unforgiveness.

These emotions are exhibited over and over in cases where

couples try to build a blended family, re-build an existing family, recover from divorce, etc. In my own life, I've had to deal with the same emotional issues we've been discussing, including those listed below.

Take a moment and review the list. Check the box that best describes how you feel, have felt recently, or may feel in the future.

☐ Shock
☐ Despair
☐ Inability to concentrate
☐ Loneliness
☐ Anger
☐ Mistrust
☐ Hatred
☐ Low self-esteem
☐ Fear

☐ Unforgiving
☐ Bitterness
☐ Feelings of depression
☐ Destructive behavior
☐ Loss of appetite
☐ Divorce
☐ Feeling Betrayed
☐ Ashamed
☐ Helpless
☐ Guilty

☐ Overwhelmed
☐ Rejection
☐ Empty
☐ Heartbroken
☐ Relieved
☐ Detached
☐ Hurt
☐ Judged

In the space provided below, write an action plan for removing the *feelings* of any unforgiveness in your life at this moment. Consider the emotions you identified above.

_____

_____

_____

_____

_____

_____

_____

_____

_____

_____

_____

_____

In the space below, begin developing a 30, 60, 90 day, or longer plan of action for addressing the steps you will take towards removing any un-forgiveness.

_____

_____

_____

_____

_____

_____

_____

_____

_____

_____

_____

The most powerful example of forgiveness is found in God's Word. Read the verse below.

Luke 23: 33–34
[33] And when they had come to the place called Calvary, there they crucified Him, and the criminals, one on the right hand and the other on the left. [34] Then Jesus said, **"Father, forgive them, for they do not know what they do."**6 *The New King James Version,* (Nashville, TN: Thomas Nelson Publishers) 1998, c1982.

Even in His death Christ had compassion, asking His Heavenly father to forgive those He never knew. Jesus gave His own life in order for us to have the opportunity of eternal life. Forgiving others is the least we can do, forgiving others is what we are required to do, considering the price that Jesus Christ paid on the cross. What will you do?

CHAPTER 10

The "Right Mix"
For Building a Strong Blended Family

In today's society it seems so important to maintain some type of "socio-status." Society's right mix for today's family is determined by career status, ranking high with our peers, financial status, etc. I found that in building a blended family, it takes time and the use of several components to form the "right mix" for pouring the foundation to build a house upon. Successful families—those that avoid the pitfalls of life, work hard at developing the "right mix" for their family foundation.

With Christ at the center of the home and working in the lives of each family member, especially mom and dad, the foundation is given added strength. Families built upon the solid rock of God's Word are given extra power to:

•trust one another
•communicate with one another
•better express themselves without being afraid of what the other might think
•show appreciation and affection for each other
•encourage one another
•spend time together and
•learn to cope with the everyday stresses of life in the blended family

Strengthening Relationships
in the Blended Family

How do we strengthen relationships within a blended family? I can tell you from experience, "Easier said than done." As I mentioned earlier, communication is the key and works as an invaluable tool for building and maintaining relationships in a blended family. Depending on the communication patterns that existed in a blended family member's original family and the extent to which the individual was exposed to conflicts, new blended family members may be unsure, or unaware of their expectations, or requirements in the new family environment.

Early on in a blended family relationship, children develop a divisive role that can greatly affect the initial process of building a blended family. The stepparent becomes an adversary, especially if the child is grieving over the loss of a previously formed family unit or if they feel guilty over the breakup of an earlier parental relationship.

In my experience I found that one of my wife's children **(whom I thought wanted the marriage more than anyone)** had hidden issues relating to his mother and me sharing time together and the attention she gave me and my children.

It is very important to communicate and keep in mind the needs of children in a blended family setting. Let me explain. I found that step and biological children often express their feelings of hurt, anger, powerlessness, fear, and rejection by lying and engaging in behavior that is aggressive, disrespectful, and even deceitful. The same child I mentioned in the previous paragraph told his mother and me how happy he was with our marriage.

Little did I know that in reality he was hurting inside, angry and furious at the thought of living with anyone other than his mother? Emotions can run very high inside the heart of a child when a mother or father considers remarrying.

Biological parents and stepparents often feel guilty when

problems with the children occur as a result of their marriage. I have been there and the feelings can be very strong.

I've met parents who considered divorcing simply because they wanted the children to be happy. It is one of the major causes of divorce in second marriages. Work on developing and laying a strong family foundation "off the bat." It is well worth the effort. Doing so gives added strength to your family.

BUILDING BLOCKS THAT FORM STRONG BLENDED FAMILIES

As I just mentioned a strong foundation is imperative if you expect to form a solid home. There are many building blocks used to build a strong and solid foundation in a blended family. Listed below are the main building blocks that I feel are essential for growth in building a blended family. The parents are responsible for installing and maintaining the building blocks listed below.

Using these blocks will reinforce the family foundation and protect against assaults from the world that might destroy a blended family's chance of survival.

☐ Prayer
☐ Love and forgiveness
☐ Commitment
☐ Appreciation and affection
☐ Positive communication
☐ Spending time together
☐ Unity

Let's look at a few of these building blocks in detail starting with prayer.

1. PRAYER

What is prayer? Webster's definition is **prayer** *n*. praying, words of worship, or entreaty to God, things prayed for.

Prayer is one of the most powerful questions for the family to consider today. Sounds like an easy task, doesn't it? Well, from experience I can again say, "Easier said than done." Almost anyone can say or recite a prayer, but it takes a fervent desire and walk with God through serving Jesus Christ to pray and pray the right way. How many times have we heard the saying "The family that prays together stays together"?

That phrase could never be truer than in today's society and yet we fail to exercise this wonderful act of freedom in our families. We need God now more than ever, and until the family realizes this, we will continue to suffer from the attacks of Satan in our homes and family lives. We will suffer and our children will as well.

THE POWER OF PRAYER

Mark 11: 22–25

[22] Then Jesus said to the disciples, "Have faith in God.

[23] I assure you that you can say to this mountain, 'May God lift you up and throw you into the sea,' and your command will be obeyed. All that's required is that you really believe and do not doubt in your heart.

[24] Listen to me! You can pray for anything, and if you believe, you will have it.

[25] But when you are praying, first forgive anyone you are holding a grudge against, so that your Father in heaven will forgive your sins, too." *New Living Translation,* (Wheaton, IL: Tyndale House Publishers, Inc.) 1996

James 5: 13–16

[13] Are any among you suffering? They should keep on

praying about it. And those who have reason to be thankful should continually sing praises to the Lord.

[14] Are any among you sick? They should call for the elders of the church and have them pray over them, anointing them with oil in the name of the Lord.

[15] And their prayer offered in faith will heal the sick, and the Lord will make them well. And anyone who has committed sins will be forgiven.

[16] Confess your sins to each other and pray for each other so that you may be healed. The earnest prayer of a righteous person has great power and wonderful results. *New Living Translation,* (Wheaton, IL: Tyndale House Publishers, Inc.) 1996

Teach your children that prayer is their link to the Heavenly Father and one of the greatest privileges we have as God's children. Share scripture verses that talk about Jesus' instructions on prayer and how prayer with God took precedence in Christ's life.

Exhort your family to turn to God before a crisis arises and to come before Him daily with praise, adoration, gratitude, and thanksgiving as well as petitions. Teach your children how to pray by consistently taking them before the throne of grace. Your faithfulness will ignite a passion for prayer in those you love most.

TEACHING THE BLENDED FAMILY TO PRAY

Several months ago, I received an e-mail from a friend of mine with information on how to teach a family to pray. This is what I received.

Decorate a plain cardboard box to look like a real mailbox (or use a discarded mailbox). Don't forget to attach a red mail flag to the outside as well. Gather your family together and hand out blank sheets of paper, pens, and business size envelopes to each person. Next, tell everyone to write down a prayer request for himself, or herself, or someone they know who is in need of prayer.

Now fold the paper and insert it into an envelope. Place all the sealed envelopes inside the mailbox. Taking turns, each family member should say a one-sentence prayer and then reach inside the mailbox and take a letter. In secret, everyone in the family should pray for the need written on his or her letter.

If you do not have a scheduled time of prayer with your family, do so as soon as possible. If the prayer is answered before the next family prayer time, write the answered prayer on a piece of paper and put it into an envelope and place inside the mailbox. Be sure to put the red flag up to alert others that mail has arrived. After dinner, ask a family member to take the envelope and read the answer to prayer aloud to the rest of the family. Say a prayer of thanksgiving to God for His faithful answer to prayers. Repeat this process each week.

PRAYER MATCH!

As a family, make a list of Bible verses according to a theme such as: love, joy, peace, patience, kindness, goodness, faithfulness, gentleness and self-control (from Galatians 5:22,23). Have family members look up verses, specifying one character quality per week, in the index of study Bibles. All prayer verses should be on a single theme during that week. Write each verse out on an index card.

Next, make a list of family members, close friends, school acquaintances, neighbors, or anyone for whom the family wants to pray. Write each of these names on separate index cards. Keep the two sets of cards in different piles. Place the verse cards in a brown paper bag. Place the name cards in a different brown paper bag.

Have each family member select one card from each bag. During the coming week, the family should pray for the person whose name they selected, using the Bible verse as their guide in praying. At the end of the week, gather together and discuss any known answers to prayer. Then mix up the cards in the bags again and repeat the process weekly.

2. LOVE AND FORGIVENESS

As mentioned in chapters eight and nine, love and forgiveness are essential in the development and strength of a blended family. Webster defines love as: strong affection, to embrace, feeling love, etc. To that we need to add respect, trust, loyalty, admiration, warmth, caring, giving, support, honesty, integrity, forgiveness and you have the "right mix" for pouring a solid foundation built on love. The greatest need in the family today is a house built on faith in Christ, love, and the ability to forgive.

Christ's love is perfect, ever enduring, and supreme. As mothers and fathers and as parents, do we express our love towards one another and our children, as we should? Do we forgive and ask for forgiveness as God instructs us to?

The words "I love you" and "forgive me" are easy to say, but do we mean them? All of us may agree that these words are a must in successfully building a blended family; however formulating the words to find the proper mix takes time and effort. I thought I had the right mix the first day my wife and I started our blended family. My assumption was that since my wife's children had no contact with their father on a full time basis, I was going to make up for that lost time and do it right. WRONG!

Building a blended family can be a massive undertaking, especially a blended family with children from both sides. Spouses **must** exhibit love and forgiveness towards one another without exception. In marriages where step-children are involved, it is extremely important to let the children know Christ is in the center of the home and through Him, Mom and Dad love each other first and foremost. **CHILDREN NEED TO SEE MOM AND DAD EXPRESSING LOVE TOWARDS ONE ANOTHER !**

I'll reference this again as mentioned in an earlier chapter, when members of a blended family see and feel the love between the husband and wife in the home, emotional stability is strengthened, and the family unit has a better chance of "coming together" sooner.

We express love in the family by developing a solid family structure beginning with:

1. Christ as the center of the home
2. The spouse next
3. Children
4. Church
5. Other family members
6. Work, etc

Love begins by entering into a relationship with God through an acceptance of Jesus Christ as ones personal Savior. It begins with each and every one of us. Let's look at what the Bible says about love?

Psalm 33: 18–22

[18] But the LORD watches over those who fear him, those who rely on his unfailing love. [19]He rescues them from death and keeps them alive in times of famine. [20]We depend on the LORD alone to save us. Only he can help us, protecting us like a shield. [21]In him our hearts rejoice, for we are trusting in his holy name. [22]Let your unfailing love surround us, LORD, for our hope is in you alone. *New Living Translation,* (Wheaton, IL: Tyndale House Publishers, Inc.) 1996

Romans 8:38 and 39

[38] And I am convinced that nothing can ever separate us from his love. Death can't, and life can't. The angels can't, and the demons can't. Our fears for today, our worries about tomorrow, and even the powers of hell can't keep God's love away. [39] Whether we are high above the sky or in the deepest ocean, nothing in all creation will ever be able to separate us from the love of God that is revealed in Christ Jesus our Lord.7 *New Living Translation,* (Wheaton, IL: Tyndale House Publishers, Inc.) 1996

Romans 13:8–10
Love Fulfills God's Requirements
[8] Pay all your debts, except the debt of love for others. You can never finish paying that! If you love your neighbor, you will fulfill all the requirements of God's law. [9] For the commandments against adultery and murder and stealing and coveting—and any other commandment—are all summed up in this one commandment: "Love your neighbor as yourself." [10] Love does no wrong to anyone, so love satisfies all of God's requirements. *New Living Translation,* (Wheaton, IL: Tyndale House Publishers, Inc.) 1996

3. COMMITMENT

It is so important to build commitment and trust between **all** members of the family, especially a blended family. No matter what the situation or family arrangement, planting seeds of commitment will produce a harvest of healthy family members.

Below are some ideas that will assist in creating a more committed family environment. It won't happen overnight, however planning, dedication, and perseverance will pay off.

Plan outside activities that devote time and energy to each other.

Children should be expected to assist around the house and perform select tasks.

Inform your family in a loving way what you as parents expect of the children and each other.

Ask each family member what they feel their duties and responsibilities are as a blended family.

Reward those who follow through assignments and tasks.

REMEMBER FUFT. . . . . Follow Up and Follow Through.

As parents, this practice will eventually pay off and set the tone for strengthening the blended family base. It will also teach children the importance of instruction, the need to complete assignments in a timely manner and the benefits of a job well done.

We are instructed in God's Word to train our children the right way; the way they should go. I said this before and repeat it again; the biological child and stepchild should be treated the same and expected to perform their assigned task like all the rest. Many parents today seem afraid to place responsibilities on their children. How else will children learn responsibility, unless we teach them?

Proverbs 22: 6
Teach your children to choose the right path, and when they are older, they will remain upon it. *New Living Translation,* (Wheaton, IL: Tyndale House Publishers, Inc.) 1996

Proverbs 22:15
[15] A youngster's heart is filled with foolishness, but discipline will drive it away. *New Living Translation,* (Wheaton, IL: Tyndale House Publishers, Inc.) 1996

Consider holidays, birthdays, etc, to be special occasions for all the family. They mean more than you realize, especially for the stepchildren. Unity through and memories are created. Decorate the house with banners in the middle of the night before birthdays and special holidays. No matter how old the family member, always do it. Don't forget Mom and Dad too.

Set family goals and don't forget the family meetings. They are very important.

I want to end this section on commitment with one very important aspect of blended family life. I found it very rewarding and beneficial to take a few minutes each night and sit down with the children to just to talk.

I have both biological and stepchildren (now my adopted children). I would go to their rooms, sit on the floor and ask them how things were going, etc. If I were talking to just one, it would not be long before the other one would come in and join us.

Boys need to connect with a strong father figure. Girls also need a strong role model; just as much, if not more. **It is so important to provide children with attention and love.**

4. APPRECIATION AND AFFECTION

Declare "appreciation" nights, when everyone around the table says something they like about the designated person. It gets the family in the habit of looking for good qualities in each other and expressing their appreciation.

Write down 10 things you like about your spouse, or children.

Many traits that irritate us are good qualities carried to the extreme. For instance, stinginess could be considered extreme thriftiness, and bossiness as leadership.

Be a good role model. Be appreciative of each other and your kids, and they'll follow suit. We hug, kiss, and say "I love you" every day. The more you hug, the more open you are about communicating.

Accept appreciation gracefully. Don't discourage praise by questioning its merit. Instead, say "Glad you like it."

5. POSITIVE COMMUNICATION

As you know I've mentioned communication several times. I cannot over emphasize the importance of keeping the lines of communication open. Keeping conversation positive versus negative and combative will enable family members to feel more respected and encourage sharing of thoughts. Don't discourage others by interrupting, mind reading, or going off on tangents. Keep a family journal. Chronicle the little things;they can mean in the most.

6. SPEND TIME TOGETHER

Quantity counts as much as quality when it comes to family togetherness. Spending quality time together as a blended family is vital for the family's survival. Quality time together is a key ingredient in building a solid foundation that supports the blended family unit. It is another part of the foundation upon which a healthy blended family identity is built upon.

Plan group activities. Reserve a night exclusively for your family. Make the time pleasant, not a time to bring up problems, create conflict.

Do nothing together can actually be doing something together. Can you remember when as a child you had some of your happiest times simply doing nothing like sitting on the porch, watching people and cars go by? The simple thing sometimes mean the most.

7. UNITY

Crisis situations usually create unity in a family and make us strong. However in blended families, it seems more difficult to achieve unity during times of trial and tribulation. Division occurs more frequently in the blended family for a variety of reasons, some have already been mentioned such as parental dispute over "my kids, your kids," disciplinary issues, the family dwelling, favoritism, etc.

So often when dividing lines are drawn as a result of family conflict, Mom and Dad take sides. Has this ever happened to you? If so you can relate to my comment. If the parents divide, the battlefield widens and the war increases. Many times the husband and wife seek to recruit those who will join their cause.

Not to say this is a bad idea, it's just very important to seek help from qualified individuals who hang out in the neutral zone, as I call it and not the immediate family zone. Choose a neutral party unrelated to any anyone in your family, making sure the person(s) have the ability to see the whole picture.

How long will the war last? Division creates an array of problems and emotions, such as stress, conflict, anger, bitterness, jealousy, etc. If we give up and quit, we fall behind in the battle for the family, allowing stress, conflict, discontentment and resentment conqueror us and win the battle. We have the power and strength to unite and defeat the forces that come against our family.

How do we unite and win the battles faced by the blended family? We achieve victory by reading, adhering to God's word and a close relationship with Jesus Christ. We have the power to wage war and defeat the enemy of the battles we face in everyday family life. Victory over family conflict and crisis is also achieved by praying, seeking God's direction in all things. Doing so creates unity.

Romans 8: 35

[35] Who shall separate us from the love of Christ? *Shall tribulation, or distress, or persecution, or famine, or nakedness, or peril, or sword? The New King James Version,* (Nashville, TN: Thomas Nelson Publishers) 1998, c1982

Romans 8: 37

[37] Yet in all these things we are more than conquerors through Him who loved us. *The New King James Version,* (Nashville, TN: Thomas Nelson Publishers) 1998, c1982

Romans 8: 38

[38] For I am persuaded that neither death nor life, nor angels nor principalities nor powers, nor things present nor things to come, *The New King James Version,* (Nashville, TN: Thomas Nelson Publishers) 1998, c1982

Romans 8: 39

[39] nor height nor depth, nor any other created thing, shall be able to separate us from the love of God which is in Christ

Jesus our Lord.*8 The New King James Version,* (Nashville, TN: Thomas Nelson Publishers) 1998, c1982

Remember these simple guidelines for dealing with conflict in the blended family:
- Pray.
- Don't allow conflict personally affect you, take control.
- Realize that disagreements aren't personal.
- Get some sleep and exercise.
- Laugh, look for the humor in any situation.
- Refocus priorities.
- Be able to forgive!
- Don't be defeated by the ills and crisis of the blended family; be a champion and crisis conqueror for Christ.

1. Is your family praying together?

O YES   O NO

If no, what do you need to do to begin praying more as a family?

_____

_____

_____

_____

_____

2. Do you express love towards your blended family members?

O YES   O NO

If you answered no, what steps will you take to better enhance your expression of love and appreciation towards members of your blended family?

_____

_____

_____

_____

_____

_____

3. How do we strengthen the blended family?

_____

_____

_____

_____

_____

4. How do you deal with the conflict in your family?

_____

_____

_____

_____

_____

5. What steps would you take to handle conflict in your family?

_____

_____

_____

_____

_____

CHAPTER 11

Children, the Wounded Warriors

Children, the innocent victims, are often caught in the crossfire of divorce and the stresses of blended family life. There can be pressure to be a "perfect family," but it takes time to get to know one another. Just getting used to each other's ways and personalities can create stress and problems for some children a blended family.

Children have to adjust more than adults realize. Things such as discipline, household rules, new expectations, the kinds of food eaten, stricter homework requirements, or household tasks children are expected to do, tend to be major areas of adjustment that cause stress. Family holidays, Christmas, and other special occasions can be hard on children as well.

Children might have to move to a new house, neighborhood, or school. It can mean losing friends and moving away from loved ones. Families combining can mean less privacy, for example, sharing a bedroom, or never having somewhere quiet to do homework or just be alone. It can be a difficult time for parents too. They have to adjust as well and may have to be a parent for a child they hardly know.

I learned through trial and error that biological children and stepchildren want to be "promoted from within." These children seek to be accepted by the biological parent and the stepparent. When a parent remarries, children can feel left out and all alone, almost "demoted" from their family position.

In a blended family children need to feel equal with other members of the family and not an outcast. This is often the case in many blended family homes. So often stepchildren feel they are on the bottom of the totem pole.

Children want to be accepted and approved by their parents, even the stepparent. You might be saying this very moment "You have no idea what my children are like, especially my step children."

How Age Affects a Child's Reaction to a Blended Family

When two people marry, both individuals need to be willing to compromise. When one or both of the spouses bring with them dependent children, compromises become more complicated. Families must decide whether they will just share living space, or will they blend into a new family unit.

Some families find forming a new blended family a fairly easy task, however for others and in most cases, challenges arise. Studies show the age of children involved in building a blended family is important. Knowing typical reactions and thoughts of different ages may teach us how to understand the way different age groups of children handle new blended family relationships.

Below are some typical reactions and thoughts of children at different ages.

Small / Preschool children:

For many small and pre-school children, divorce is seldom final. Because they believe their family may one day be reunited, remarriage may be a threat. Did you know that many young children carry guilt and thoughts such as, "Daddy left because I didn't make my bed," or, "If I had helped more, Mommy would not have gone away."

Parents can help by being sensitive to a child's feelings, frequently reassuring and listening to them. Know and understand that a young child's feelings are common and not easily dispelled. Reassurance and love is extremely important in the life of a small child.

On the other hand, preschoolers adjust relatively easily to having two homes and two sets of rules. A young child's view and idea of time is very limited to themselves, "forever" is "tomorrow." They may be afraid and have a fear of being abandoned, or losing their other parent in the remarriage. As long as they are reassured of the love of both parents, they can handle most changes fairly well.

We should let our children know it is okay to love the stepparent. However, do not insist on immediate love. Assure them it is possible to love both parents and stepparents. It is harmful to make a small (or any child) choose between important people in their lives.

CHILDREN BETWEEN THE AGES OF 6–10:

This age group of children tends to express their feelings by hiding them inside, At home and around other people as well. These children express their emotions by feeling alone and often fail at school or other activities. Children in this age group often feel everything is out of control. Give them some freedom in choosing what clothes and hairstyles to wear or how their rooms are arranged and kept. Be careful though, to much freedom can lead to problems. Remember you are still the parent and still in control. Parents govern the home not the children. Set standards and guidelines on how far they can go. You standards will assist in preparing children for the future.

Remarriage sends the message to children that their biological parents will not get back together. Talk to the children, reaffirm your love towards them and provide them with opportunities to sit and discuss their concerns and feelings. Their feelings are very important.

CHILDREN BETWEEN THE AGES OF 11–12:

Children at this age begin to pull away from the family. They are beginning to test their independence. They still need the security of knowing that the family is there for support when they need it, however, most children want to spread their wings and grow up fast but without the responsibilities that go along with growing up. Part of a parent's job at this stage is to help children by guiding them along the way. Show concern and encourage communication often.

TEENAGERS 13–19:

In single-parent families, many teens and adolescents take on adult roles. They become part of the decision-making process and are frequently given responsibility for themselves and siblings. This encourages them to think for themselves as adults. Many teenagers resent giving up these rights and to some degree responsibilities when a parent remarries.

Open, honest communication can help pinpoint some of those tasks they want to continue. Parents may feel it necessary to develop methods of including the teenagers in the decision making process which will positively affect their roles in the blended family and future relationships. Be open to allowing the children to have more input on issues and concerns in the family. By allowing the children to take on responsibilities, assist in the decision making process, trust, improved self esteem and a feeling of self worth is created which makes them feel like an important part of the family.

TRYING TO UNDERSTAND TEENAGERS IN A BLENDED FAMILY

Its one thing to try and understand a teenager in a traditional family, but it becomes a completely different "ball game" to try and understand the emotions of a teen in a blended family.

One thing that most parents and stepparents of teenagers want is a better relationship with their teens.

As children continue to grow and change, often the parent-teen relationship suffers. This doesn't have to be the case. With a little effort, parents can stay connected to their teens during the initial stages of blended family development and beyond.

There are many ways to build a better relationship with teenagers, but I've found that if you follow the basic steps listed below, you will begin to see the building of a firm foundational relationship, that may very well surprise you.

RESPECT

Respect is the first step to improving any relationship, teenager or, adult. The job God has given us as parents and stepparents is to provide guidance and discipline for our teenagers, but we also have the responsibility to treat our teens with respect (1 Peter 2:17). While the parent and child have different roles and responsibilities in the family, no one should be considered more important than any other.

You show respect when you treat your teen like an equal. This doesn't mean that you both have the same authority and function in the family, but it does mean that you are both God's children and deserve respect. While one of our roles as a parent is to guide our teens, we need to do this respectfully.

HAVE FUN

The next step to take is to have fun with your teen. The Bible is not silent about the importance of joy in our lives. In fact, Nehemiah 8:10 tells us the "joy of the Lord is our strength." As teenagers enter high school, time with them should be considered precious. With high school sports, studies, friends, and extra-curricular activities, there isn't much time left for connecting as a family.

Having fun with your teenager is important and it doesn't need to take much of your time. It can be as simple as sharing a meal together, renting a video to watch together, or driving together in a car. Just remember to make some memories.

GIVE ENCOURAGEMENT

Become an encouragement to your children in your blended family. Feeling capable and worthy of being loved is extremely important to children. Make sure you point out their unique qualities, putting more emphasis on their strengths instead of their weaknesses.

LOVE

Remember to show teenagers and all the children in your family love. So important and yet so many parents forget to express this foundational element. Though they are no longer children, teens still need to feel that their parents love them. Show them you love them with both words and actions. Tell them you love them, give them hugs, and pats on the backs, just do something special for them and all the children.

Building a better relationship with your teenager may take work, but it is definitely worth the effort.

CHILDREN AND THEIR NEEDS IN THE BLENDED FAMILY

Now that we have looked at the different age categories of children, let's take a moment and look at the needs of children in a blended family setting. Understanding and taking into account the developmental levels and needs of the children entering into a blended family can provide insight in to some of the particularly sensitive issues. For example, the relationship between a child and a new stepparent will generate a special need to be aware of and requires attention with boundaries.

It can be very helpful for the stepparents of a child to have a support group of other parents and stepparents with whom to discuss parenting problems.

It also helps for the parent and stepparent to have a clear appreciation of the temperaments and coping skills of the children in the stepfamily. Some children are temperamentally better equipped than others to handle transitions, and become less emotionally aroused and distressed by expected or unexpected frustrations and disappointments.

Some children can be emotionally sensitive and over reactive when blended families are formed. Children in this category need more time to deal with the emotional frustrations associated with blended family life and its development. A longer period of adjustment can be expected in the more emotional sensitive child.

It is important to remember that although a child may appear to be " doing just fine" in adjusting to their new blended family life, they too at times can feel overwhelmed and held captive by the emotions associated with being part of a new blended family.

ADJUSTING TO CHANGE

It is not an overstatement to say that each family situation is unique and that there are no general rules or guidelines that will guarantee positive outcomes in parenting, especially when helping children cope with change. We know that even positive changes are stressful for both children and adults, and the stress becomes even greater when negative emotions are generated.

We also know that there is a tendency to underestimate the amount of time it will take to adjust to change, that some of us are uncomfortable with strong negative emotions and may deny or minimize them, and that it is unusual for a parent to wish to deliberately cause distress to a child.

There are many situations and contributing factors that could interfere with the natural expectations of building a blended family, particularly the areas of adjustment when the "blending" feels more like grinding. Working at and resolving difficulties in the formation of a new family unit takes time, patience and a determined resolve. This will help parents and stepparents maintain their sense of humor and perspective during the building process.

To this point you have read information and had presented to you guidelines to assist in building and strengthening your blended family. As I worked on the final stages of this book I struggled regarding whether or not to include what you are about to read. My decision was based on allowing you the reader of this book to see first hand from the author's pen that he too has experienced trials (some extreme as you will soon read) and challenges discussed and referenced in his book.

Here are two real life heart wrenching stories that I have first hand knowledge of. I did not ask to go through them, but it happened. My purpose in sharing these personal stories with you is three fold.

1) To encourage you in the event you encounter extreme challenges in your blended family.
2) To let you know there is hope no matter what you face and
3) More importantly with God all things are possible.

What you read may shock and even surprise you. I ask that you carefully consider the stories. These are trying situations that occurred not long after my wife and I were married. The stories are gripping, challenging and true. These are real life dramas ones you might see, or hear on a prime time television program. It is a story of two teenagers struggle with life, the changes and challenges brought about as a result of separation, divorce, remarriage and adjusting to a new family. This first story is about my now adopted son, Josh, and the second story is concerning my biological daughter, Jenna.

Josh's Story

Its 9pm, Wednesday December 9th, 1998 only 3 weeks after my wife and I were married. I just finished a conversation with my stepson Josh in our kitchen. I am in shock after hearing a confession that you would only hear in the movies, or a television documentary. I can feel my heart beat as though it is on the verge of exploding, my hands are shaking, I am sweating and can hardly speak. What do I tell Marie? What do I say to her? How do I break the news, do I call the police or not? What do I do!!

Now you are going to read one of the most unexpected events I or anyone else could ever expect in a blended family. Prior to his confession and statements, Josh made a point to tell me that I would never guess what he had done. As he was trying to explain things, I was working very hard not to show my stirring emotions. I tried to act as though it was not a big deal, however deep down inside my stomach was churning. I began to guess what it was he had done.

First I said "did you get a girl pregnant"?, No it's worse than that he replied. Did you get caught shoplifting?, Did you rob a bank? Did you get caught with drugs. Again he said no. Then I asked jokingly did you kill someone?

A silence engulfed the room and Josh's eyes became as arrows piercing my soul. He looked at me with this face of cold steel and replied yes I did. Although Josh didn't know it, my stomach fell to my knees. Trying to maintain my composure, I looked back at him as though to say "so what," then added "when did it happen and who was the person?

Josh began to explain that a couple of years earlier he was connected to gang. He proceeded to explain that one night while still involved in the gang he met a young man approximately 17 years of age in a park and shot him point blank with a 9mm Glock hand gun. His details were perfect and to the tee. You couldn't help but believe his story.

As Josh left the room he asked that I not tell anyone, especially his mother. As he walked away I collapsed to the floor in tears weeping silently. What would you do as a new husband and stepfather after hearing what I did? All the joy of my new marriage and life seemed to vanish instantly. All the plans for building my new family are now covered by this dark cloud. Why would Josh tell me this? Was he lying and if so why?

Josh was the one that wanted his mother and I to marry.

I slowly stepped to the room where my wife lay sleeping. I carefully got in the bed and began to pray. After praying I rolled over placed my arms around my wife and asked her if she was awake. To my surprise she was. She asked me what Josh and I talked about. Although I promised Josh I would not tell anyone, I had to tell my wife. What would you do? Tell your wife, or keep your promise? Step children need and seek trust from their new step parents, but where do you draw the line. Was this secret worth revealing? If it did happen then there is a mother out there somewhere who needs to know who killed her son. WHAT DO I DO?

If I remained silent, am I as guilty as Josh? As I pondered what to do I was reminded of my promise to Marie and that was I would never keep anything from her, nothing. I proceeded to tell Marie what I heard from Josh. She layed in the bed still and began to breath heavily and then the tears began to flow. She couldn't believe what I was telling her. I could sense her emotions roll to the edge. She looked at me with a fear I have never seen in a person before and said "what do we do, do you think he did it"?

All I could say was I don't know, but his story was very convincing. Marie wanted to know do we call the police, or what? We decided to wait until morning to make our decision. The next day we had nothing on our minds but the previous nights events.

We did not call the police for several days. Instead we decided to wait and see if Josh had told his story to someone else.

The Police get involved!!

The day came when I received a phone call that would bring this part of our nightmare to an end. A phone call was received informing me that Josh had confessed to someone other than me. This time a call would be made to the police by an anonymous parent who overheard their daughter talking about Josh's confession over the phone.

In few days Josh would be picked up by the police and transported to jail for questioning. Little did we know at the time that a murder (resembling the one Josh stated he committed) took place in the next county. Before we knew it, my wife and I were being questioned, or should I say interrogated by local law enforcement officials. I could not believe what was happening. Why was I here? God please help me!!

After 6 hours of interrogation with various law enforcement officials, my wife and I were told that they did not believe Josh killed anyone. They were convinced Josh made up the story in an attempt to separate my wife and I. Why would the very person who was for our marriage, now be against it?

This would be just one of the many trials and tests of our faith to come. Without going into detail, we would face many challenges with Josh, including a drug addiction and entering him into different rehabilitation facilities. It was our faith in God, the love we had for one another, our love for Josh and perseverance that won out.

Our fight to save Josh was one my wife and I were determined not to lose. Now he lives in freedom. When situations like this arise in blended families, the first course of action is a defensive one, especially when the child in question is not yours. For me I had to love Josh as my own and I will admit, at times it was not easy. I soon learned Josh was jealous and all the talk of his approval of me and marrying his mother was a nothing more than a band aid on a wound getting ready to burst open.

One of the greatest gifts I received from my wife during this time was her support of me. She was also a prime example of tough love. I saw a woman newly remarried facing the biggest challenge of her life. She chose to stand beside her new husband and not give in to the pressures generated by the "biological connection" I mentioned in an earlier chapter. The operative word here is commitment!

When individuals remarry it is important to let the children know the importance of a husband and wife supporting one another through commitment.

I remember my wife telling police detectives interrogating Josh that if he did commit a crime he should go to jail. The statement she made shocked everyone, including me. She stated that if Josh did take the life of another, then there was a mother out there hurting and we needed to do what was right. We would still stand beside Josh no matter what the outcome.

This is a great example to everyone reading this story. It took our faith in God, communication, commitment, developing an action plan consisting of daily conversations with Josh, making sure we knew where he was, who his friends were, and letting him know we loved and supported him. Children want their parents to be proud of them, especially when the male biological parent is not in the picture. Men contribute more than they realize to the emotional well being of children.

Through all the trials and heartache, it was our desire to show our children the importance of keeping a family together. Our fervent desire as husband and wife and a resolve not to give in to defeat when our backs seemed pressed against the wall were key elements in winning the battle we faced!

We fought for Josh's freedom from drugs, alcohol abuse, and anger, and won. Now he fights for the freedom of our country…what a miracle!

This is Josh today. He is married, serving our country in the Army, has a beautiful wife and beautiful children and is on track with his life.

I am very proud of Josh Collins. Not my adopted son…my son, our hero.

Sidenote: in the early days of our

blended family, Josh struggled with the question of how I could I love him. After all, I wasn't his biological dad. Here is the coolest thing: when Josh got married, his wife had a daughter from a previous relationship.

Now Josh is just like me. He too has a blended family and adopted his wife's daughter, whom he loves dearly. It's interesting how things come full circle for the best. Now Josh can understand how I was able to love him. I believe everything happens for a reason. It prepared Josh for the role of husband, father, provider and the greatest of all titles: Dad!

James says it well in the book of James chapter1: verses 2–4 (NIV):

[2]Consider it pure joy, my brothers, whenever you face trials of many kinds, [3]because you know that the testing of your faith develops perseverance. [4]Perseverance must finish its work so that you may be mature and complete, not lacking anything.

The scripture says it very well, yet at times it is easier to read than actually go through trials and testing. But when we do and persevere we become the victors and not the victims.

Jenna's Story

Below is Jenna's story. I know this young lady; she is my daughter. Read carefully as she retraces one of the most challenging episodes in her life. The events in her life occurred one year after my wife and I were married. As with Josh's story you will see too that God was in control of Jenna's life as well. This is her story.

I really don't think of myself as anything more than an average teenager. I hope sharing my story can be useful to someone, especially teenagers or children in your home. I'm seventeen and a senior in high school. I have been living with my dad and step mom for over a year. I grew up with my mother, brother, and sister, rarely seeing my dad. My parents divorced when I was in second grade or so, and I know it's cliché, but it did have an incredible impact.

You don't think it will affect you, but even years later, you can trace back to it as the root of some problems. From that point on, I felt abandoned by my dad and withdrew from any of his attempts to get closer to me. My mother always put him down, she never told me when he called and said he didn't love me.

All I saw for years was bitterness from my mother towards my dad. Girls need their fathers! I felt really alone, like nobody understood me, and the only thing that helped was reading. When I reached middle school and boys started showing an interest in me, it was like a light went on. It made me feel oddly secure knowing boys thought I was pretty or wanted to "make out" with me.

I strongly believe every little girl should be told she's pretty and worth something, beginning at a young age. Children need that. When girls grow up with low self-esteem, they find temporary approval in the wrong places. Once I was in high school, I continued on a downward spiral. Looking back, it's easy to see where I could have been helped and where I went wrong. I was reaching out, but everyone else was caught up in his or her own problems. I didn't want to bother them; I just wished they had noticed.

My freshman year, I started having panic attacks and showing signs of Obsessive Compulsive Disorder (OCD) and depression. Looking at me from an outsider's point of view, I looked normal. I'd always been able to hide my problems well.

That same year, on November 14, 1998, my dad married my step mom, and I gained four new stepbrothers. But at the time, I was so deep in my own pity I didn't want to get to know any of them. I was reaching out to my mother, but she didn't care to notice the signs of my problem. She had her own life to deal with.

My mother was pregnant, she got married, and my brother and sister and I left our home and moved into my stepfather's house. I just wished we could have moved to a new house and started all over together. The summer before my sophomore year was one of the worst few months I've ever had. Anyone with OCD (oppressive compulsive disorder), depression, or an anxiety disorder knows it's impossible to describe the chaos in your mind, especially a with a new family. My own struggles seemed even greater. Unless you have experienced it, you can't know what I'm talking about. OCD is like you're in a prison, and all day you do nothing but torture yourself.

When I had the tiniest scratch, I would go hysterical thinking it was cancer or some fatal disease, and I made my mom take me to the doctor every week. I was so scared of dying, but I never knew why. I was put on medicine for the OCD and panic, and eventually they calmed me down. My sophomore year seemed better, and I found if I kept busy, I didn't have as many panic attacks. But then it happened.

That January, school was out for two weeks because of snow. All of a sudden, I became extremely depressed. I would sit in my room for days and not eat or shower or speak to anyone. All I could do was cry; still no one noticed I was reaching out. Why? When someone would try to talk to me, I would yell at them and be so mean they would leave. Once school returned, I managed to keep the feelings under control.

I started dating someone in March, and my mom didn't approve. She wouldn't talk to me. I wanted my dad, but mom said he didn't care and was not going to let me see him. I needed him so much, but when he called, I wouldn't talk to him. I ignored my mom and kept seeing this guy I was dating. He was the only one that cared for me, but my mom eventually found out I was still seeing him.

I lost it one day at school, and decided I hated life so much I would end it. I stole a knife from the home economics department and went to the bathroom and in frenzy started cutting my arms. A teacher came in and grabbed me and took me to a room where she got me bandages and called my mom. My mom came to take me to the hospital, she was mad at me. So I ran and hid in a room, and they sent the school deputy to find me, which of course she did. So I went to the hospital and got shots, answered questions, and got to go home. I didn't go back to school for a few days.

That night my mom called my dad and told him what had happened. She didn't want to deal with me anymore. My dad called me, talked with me and he came to see me the next day. I was trying to figure out why my dad was concerned and why my mother didn't mind him coming now when she tried so hard for years to keep him away. I was about to learn how much I needed my dad and that he did love me.

That summer I went to live with my dad and step mom. I decided to stay and go to school there. It was hard at first leaving my friends. I was still depressed some, but taking my medication. There was still pain inside me and on a few occasions, I cut myself again. There was such a release in making myself bleed. It was the only thing that would relieve the internal pain. A couple of times my parents would see my arms cut, but they had no idea what to do. I tried to make them think I was okay. Depression is the most horrible black cloud that covers your whole life.

On September 2000, it happened again, but the course of events about to take place would change my life forever. This is what happened:

I went to the bathroom at school (my new one) and once again cut my arms and thighs. My counselor called my dad; he came to the school, picked me up and made a decision to seek help for me. He took me to the local hospital and I saw some people. I know it was hard on my dad and I could see the pain in his eyes.

My dad, talked with several medical and mental health professionals. My dad made a decision that would change my life. He found a psychiatric hospital in Greensboro, NC for kids, where I was admitted and spent five days there. I met a lot of kids like me and I began to realize how lucky I was. My dad and step mom came to see me every day. My dad would ask the nurses and counselors when I would be stable. My dad and stepmom cried and looked so hurt. I knew that my dad loved me, and I saw that. When the going was tough, he was the one really there for me.

It really hurt me to see that they cared so much for me and how upset they were to see what I was going through. For the first time, I knew my dad really loved me. I eventually got to leave, and I have never been so happy to see fried food and a drink a Mountain Dew. They got me on a regular schedule for my medicine, started taking me to church, and there I gave my heart and life to Jesus. So I have begun my journey back to the sane, and I am happy to say I am there now with peace and joy in my heart.

My dad and stepmom love each other and I know that, but I know kids worry them sometimes. My dad adopted all four of my stepbrothers, and I think of them as my real brothers and consider my stepmother a mom. It was hard for them to get past some issues that surround blended families, but I have seen miracles take place. I love my family so much, and I am so grateful I have all my brothers and sisters.

My stepmom has been an unbelievable blessing. She has helped me tremendously and I really don't differentiate between genetically related and stepfamily. I now have a relationship with my dad, and I admire him so much. I know he is trying to be the husband and father God wants him to be, and in my opinion he's succeeded.

Blended families are hard to make work, but if God is the center of the home, like ours, they will work. Both parents have to love one another, not show favoritism, be fair, and treat all the kids the same.

I am fortunate enough to have never had a problem in feeling bitter towards my stepbrothers—really my bonus brothers.

Parents can make or break a family and as my dad says, I say that "Parents CAN MAKE, OR BREAK A CHILD."

There are still challenges, but with Jesus in my heart, I will survive. Love your family and keep it together no matter what.

Jenna Faith Collins

If we made it through what you just read, you too can face any trial, test, or tribulation.

Update: Jenna is in college, taking medication for her panic attacks. She no longer resorts to self mutilation to release her pain she once felt and is working hard to live an active fulfilling life.

Our other 5 children are also working hard and leading productive lives.

1. Tony – married, working for a major corporation and playing in a band that recently signed a major record deal
2. Shane – in the Marines and serving our country like his brother Josh
3. Blake – living in Texas, attending bible college working on becoming a missionary, or pastor
4. Aaron – living in Texas, working for a major corporation and involved in church
5. Lindsey – living in NC, attending college

WHAT CHILDREN REALLY NEED FROM THEIR PARENTS

Children need love, compassion, understanding, appreciation, including the need for their parents, stepparents and other individuals to be proud of them. A tremendous aspect of molding a child's character and building confidence is when we as adults, moms, dads, step-moms, step-dads, tell them how proud we are of them.

A hug and pat on the back and sincerely saying the words, "I'm proud of you," will go a long way in solidifying a blended family.

Children also need and want discipline, believe it or not. Ask the children in your home the things they really need from you. My daughter gave me the following list of things you might be surprised to hear teenagers say they want and need. You too might be surprised at what you are about to read.

- Set limits for me. I know quite well that I ought not to have all I ask for. I am only testing you.
- Be firm with me. I prefer it. It lets me know where I stand.
- Lead me rather than force me. If you force me, it teaches me that power is all that counts. I will respond more readily to being led.
- Be consistent. Inconsistency confuses me and makes me try harder to get away with everything I can.
- Make promises that you will be able to keep. That will encourage my trust in you.
- Remember that I am being provocative when I say and do things just to upset you. If you fall for my provocation, I win and I'll try for more such victories.
- Keep calm when I say, "I hate you." I don't mean it; I just want you to feel sorry for what you have done to me.
- Let me do the things that I can do for myself. If you do them for me, it makes me feel like a baby, and I may continue to put you in my service.
- Correct me in private. I'll take much more notice if you talk quietly with me in private rather than with other people present.
- Discuss my behavior when the conflict has subsided. In the heat of conflict for some reason my hearing is not very good and my cooperation is even worse. It is all right for you to take the action required, but let's not talk about it until later.
- Talk with me rather than preach to me. You'd be surprised how well I know what's right and wrong.

- •Help me feel that my mistakes are not sins. I have to learn to make mistakes without feeling that I am no good.
- •Talk firmly without nagging. If you nag, I shall protect myself by appearing deaf.

We've mentioned several times throughout the Building a Blended Family study how important prayer is. This is one area in a blended family and a Christian's life that *cannot* be neglected. Prayer and reading the Bible are key elements in developing a closer relationship with God through His Son Jesus Christ. Prayer is the key ingredient found in the recipe for keeping the blended family strong.

In the blended family, prayer gives us strength to handle the everyday stresses and issues we face.

Through prayer we receive power and wisdom from on high, allowing for a continued closer walk with the Heavenly Father and strength to deal with the challenges brought about by children in the blended family setting.

We *must not* and *cannot* become complacent in our prayer life, or in the manner in which we pray.

God wants a sincere heart, one filled with the desire to be like Christ. There is joy, peace and happiness for those who pray and fervently seek the Father through a personal relationship with Christ. More than ever before, it is imperative that we pray for our children, especially those in a blended family setting. Prayer with our spouse and children must be a daily routine and a top priority, without exception.

In my research on blended families, I found the following outline for daily prayer with the family:

DAILY PRAYER SUGGESTIONS FOR CHILDREN IN A BLENDED FAMILY

MONDAY:

Ask God to place a protective, solid hedge around your

children so that Satan cannot reach in and lead them into temptation and so they will be safe from harm. Parents should practice and instruct their children on the scripture found in James 4:7, 2 Thessalonians 3:3; and Psalm 33:20.

TUESDAY:

Pray that your children would use godly wisdom in selecting friends and peers that will make a positive difference in their lives. Ask God to give each child a discernment of people as well as knowing the difference between right and wrong. Proverbs 1:10; 18:24; Deuteronomy 13:6, 8.

WEDNESDAY:

Pray that your children would stay pure in their thoughts and deeds. Psalm 24:4–5; Job 17:9.

THURSDAY:

Pray that they will be caught if they wander into cheating, lies, or mischief. Hebrews 13:18–19.

FRIDAY:

Pray they will be alert and thinking clearly as they attend school and extra curricular activities and as they take exams. Ask God to help them be motivated to do the best they are capable of doing. Colossians 3:17; 1 Corinthians 10:31.

SATURDAY:

Pray for the spouse each child will marry someday. Ask that they will come from godly homes and have an appetite to live the spiritual truth they've learned. Pray also that their goals and purpose will be the same as your own children and their future homes would be godly. Deuteronomy 5:29.

SUNDAY:

Ask God to help them live their lives for Him and that He will use them as a testimony and witness for His glory. Pray that they'll be grown to full spiritual maturity. Psalms 78:1–8, 103:17–18; Isaiah 54:13; Ephesians 3:20–21.

The greatest shield of protection we as parents and stepparents can provide for our children is prayer. It's never too late to start. 1 Samuel 12:23; James 5:16; Colossians 4:2.

1. What do you feel your children and, or stepchildren need from you?

_____

2. As a parent, what do you need to do for your children/stepchildren to provide them with a more secure family environment?

_____

CHAPTER 12

Stress and the Blended Family

I would agree that stress is a major factor in how act, react, and address issues in our life. Stress affects us in many ways. We can control it or allow it to conquer us. How to deal with stress in the blended family is very important. It would be rare, almost impossible to find a family, especially a blended family free from the stressors of life that affect us all.

Below are the some signs and symptoms of stress. You will also find a simple stress reduction plan.

SIGNS OF STRESS!

The emotional, physiological and physical signs of stress are . . .
- muscles feel tight
- body aches
- nervous twitches in the eyelids
- restlessness
- sleeplessness
- clearing your throat
- frequent colds
- upset stomach
- sweating
- itchy skin, or rashes
- stiff posture
- holding things tightly

•strong startle response
•headaches
•high blood pressure
•stuttering and stumbling over words
•poor attention span
•excessive worrying
•preoccupation with a certain situation
•walking or talking faster
•obsessive thoughts
•compulsive actions
•unexplained outbursts of emotions
•excessive, or bad dreams
•always in a hurry
•irritation when delayed
•feeling panicked
•feeling anxious
•getting tongue-tangled, avoiding people
•nervous habits
•changing habits (becoming less or more organized)
•inability to remember things
•feeling confused
•holding grudges against people
•irritability, snappy at people
•crying

Consider the following:

•Are you often tense, uptight, and unable to relax?
•Do setbacks in your life bother you?
•Do you bypass simple pleasures in life?
•Do you worry?
•Do you doubt yourself and suffer from low self-esteem?
•Does you find yourself getting angry more often than you
  use to?
•Do you have trouble sleeping?

•Are you tired and feeling sluggish?
•Do you feel the weight of the world on your shoulder?

If you answered yes to any one of the questions listed above, it is quite possible that you could be over-stressed.

If you answered yes to more than 5 of the questions listed above, then your risk of being highly stressed has doubled. Now the question is, "what do I do? The answer is very simple.

STRESS RELIEF FROM A BIBLICAL PERSPECTIVE

Stress will disappear and dissolve when we acknowledge our dependence upon God and submit to His will and leadership. Psalm 73: 26

In 1st Peter chapter 5, verses 6 and 7 we read:
⁶Therefore humble yourselves under the mighty hand of God that He may exalt you in due time, ⁷casting all your care upon Him, for He cares for you.

Knowing, believing and understanding that God cares for us will be the key factor in dealing with stress in the blended family, stress in our daily lives, or shall we say just life in general.

Psalm 37: 3–7
³*Trust* in the LORD, and do good; Dwell in the land, and feed on His faithfulness. ⁴*Delight* yourself also in the LORD, And He shall give you the desires of your heart ⁵*Commit* your way to the LORD, *Trust* also in Him, And He shall bring it to pass. ⁶He shall bring forth your righteousness as the light, And your justice as the noonday. ⁷*Rest* in the LORD, and wait patiently for Him; ***Do not fret*** because of him who prospers

in his way, Because of the man who brings wicked schemes to pass.

Look at the key words in the scripture you just read and consider their meaning. They are:

Do not fret, other words do not become vexed or worried

Trust in God, be assured and rely on the His character, ability and strength, knowing that your confidence is placed in Him.

Commit all that you do unto the Lord and acknowledge Him as your source of strength.

Rest in the freedom found in God's word and the Love He has for you.

Methods in dealing with stress

Step number one:
The way and methods in which we handle stress in the blended family is very important to understand. Take a piece of paper and list the things in your life, or blended family that you feel causes stress. Discuss these with your spouse and family.

Step number two:
Review the items below carefully. Remember and implement those items that you feel could assist in dealing with the stressors in your life.

- Practice "stress switching." If I'm unsuccessful at balancing my checkbook, setting it aside and worrying about it does me no good. Instead, I "stress switch," replacing a stressful activity with something positive, such as exercise, so I can return and tackle the problem refreshed.
- Exercise. I know, it's hard to find time for it. But you'll discover more energy and efficiency when you make even simple exercise a priority.

- Establish stability zones. It can be a favorite place for prayer, an enjoyable routine, or an annual vacation spot.
- Play music. When God created music, he somehow enabled it to penetrate straight to the depths of our spirit.
- Breathe deeply. This simple "8–8-8" breathing exercise is low-tech but effective: Inhale slowly on an 8 count, hold for another 8, then exhale slowly on 8.
- Practice saying NO. Take lessons from a two year old. Saying no is not an excuse for noninvolvement, laziness, or insensitivity. It's simply living by our priorities.
- Limit time with negative people. They drain your energy. You can't satisfy or change them—and it will exhaust you to try.
- Simplify meal choices. "Plan meals with your family's likes and dislikes in mind,"
- Adjust expectations. If you always expect success, you're destined to be chronically frustrated. But if you expect life to be messy, you're more likely to be content with the simple blessings God sends your way.
- Develop healthy sleeping habits. Choose to get enough sleep. Value it. Take a nap—and don't feel guilty.
- Learn to laugh. One person, after a hurricane in southern Florida devastated her house, posted a sign in the front yard: "Open House." It didn't help her rebuild, but it helped her weather the storm.
- Choose daily to follow God. Moses reminded people to choose carefully: "Choose life, so that you and your children may live, and that you may love the Lord your God, listen to his voice, and hold fast to him" **(Deuteronomy 30:19–20).**

A SAMPLE STRESS ACTION PLAN:

- •Look for humor and don't take yourself too seriously.
- •Keep a journal.
- •Don't take everything friends and relatives say at face value.
- •Cultivate a positive attitude towards friends and relatives.
- •Get enough sleep and exercise.
- •Eat a well-balanced diet.
- •Keep the proper perspective.
- •Study Gods word and. . . .
- **•PRAY/STUDY the Bible**

The ability to handle and deal with the stresses we face in life is to approach our stresses with the confidence in knowing that God is our source of strength, He is in control and cares for you and me.

CHAPTER 13

Change the Trend, "Go Against the Grain"

As you conclude reading Building a Blended Family, I can't over emphasize the importance of keeping our blended families together. Many in society look at the blended family as nothing more than another group of people.

Building a blended family is a journey, consisting of many roads. In my own situation, I found that building a blended family is a **process**, not an event and takes time. It consists of love and understanding that children in a blended family setting adjust more easily when the parents co-parent together, seeking God's direction in all things. It is also important that the biological mother and father communicate one with another putting away their own differences and agenda and putting their children first, learning to forgive one another.

If and when conflict or disagreement arises, don't look at it as failure. Take the opportunity to learn and grow from it. For all you know, it could be an opportunity to address and prevent a problem before it becomes conflict, or a major family road block. Did you know that blended families can use trials, problems, and crisis situations to move to the next level toward making positive decisions and changes that will strengthen their families and interpersonal relationships?

Husbands and wives, step moms and step dads, your relationships are vital and so important in keeping your blended family together. More importantly however is your relationship with God. It must be without doubt the focal point in all you do. By seeking God in all things, your blended family will become stronger, thereby preventing you from giving into to the destructive schemes of our society and world.

Will you change the trend of today's family and go against the grain, making your blended family strong? The trials and conflicts that come against our blended families *will* make us or destroy us.

On September 11th, 2001 the largest attack against America occurred. In a speech delivered by President George W. Bush shortly after the attack on September 11th, twelve words were spoken that I shall never forget. The words **"We will not tire. We will not falter. We will not fail."** rang out proclaiming our resolve and determination to rebuild and recover from this horrific attack on our country.

Days later I kept returning to the words our President spoke. I began to think about how our family has been attacked by the terrorist of greed, money, divorce, materialism, sex, drugs, alcoholism and power.

Satan, the Christian's enemy is attacking the family in one last effort to destroy what God has put together. He knows he is a defeated foe, yet continues on in a relentless effort to destroy the family, steal as much as he can from us and ruin as many lives as possible before his final day, which is coming very soon.

But praise God!, we have the power through His Son, Jesus Christ to go to the enemies camp and take back what he has stolen from us.

THE WHOLE ARMOR OF GOD

How do we win? We win by wearing God's armor **(His Word)** and living the life Christ reveals to us. God makes us a promise: "When you pass through the waters, I will be with you; and when you pass through the rivers, they will not sweep over you. When you walk through the fire, you will not be burned; the flames will not set you ablaze." (Isaiah 43:2)

Below are key scriptures in winning the war against the things that come against us as we travel this life and build a blended family.

Ephesians: 6:10–17

[10] Finally, my brethren, be strong in the Lord and in the power of His might.

[11] Put on the whole armor of God, that you may be able to stand against the wiles of the devil.

[12] For we do not wrestle against flesh and blood, but against principalities, against powers, against the rulers of the darkness of this age, against spiritual hosts of wickedness in the heavenly places.

[13] Therefore take up the whole armor of God, that you may be able to withstand in the evil day, and having done all, to stand.

[14] Stand therefore, having girded your waist with truth, having put on the breastplate of righteousness, [15] and having shod your feet with the preparation of the gospel of peace;

[16] above all, taking the shield of faith with which you will be able to quench all the fiery darts of the wicked one.

[17] And take the helmet of salvation, and the sword of the Spirit, which is the word of God; *The New King James Version,* (Nashville, TN: Thomas Nelson Publishers) 1998, c1982.

Trust God for all things, striving to keep Jesus Christ first in your life and your blended family's life. By placing Jesus Christ first in your life, marriage and home, you *will be* more than a conqueror and you will have the ability to overcome any obstacle, trial, trouble, or tribulation your blended family may face.

REMEMBER THE FOLLOWING WORDS; USE THEM AS YOUR BLENDED FAMILY'S MOTTO . . .

In the name of Jesus Christ, "We will not tire, We will not falter, We will not fail."

PARENTS, STEPPARENTS, THE CHOICE IS YOURS, WHAT WILL YOU DO?

Now that you have completed Building a Blended Family, I trust you have received some insight into the issues, or questions regarding blended family life. A personal relationship with Jesus Christ is the real answer to the questions and problems we face in developing a blended family, including hope, peace, contentment, joy, forgiveness and everlasting life.

Accepting Jesus Christ as your Savior gives you a peace that surpasses anything the world can offer or give. There will be times when the storms clouds still arise, the winds blow, and the sea becomes rough, but rest assured if you allow Jesus to be the captain of your life, you can face the trials and storms of life with peace and joy.

I know that without Jesus at the helm, I would have ship wrecked many times. There is nothing the world can offer, or supply that will take the place of accepting, knowing, and serving God through a personal relationship with Jesus Christ.

As you read this book, you may feel your heartstrings being pulled. You may be asking yourself questions about your relationship with God. Do you really know Him? **Now I have a question for you. Listen very carefully. This is the most important question you will ever be asked.** If you died today and stood before God would He say enter in my good and faithful servant, or would He say depart from me for I never knew you?

The Lord wants you to come home today, right now at this very moment. Think of your children and family. I want to share the words my daughter wrote in a letter to me several years ago when her mother and I separated. This sweet little girl wanted nothing more than for her daddy to come home. She was 6 years old.

Dear daddy, please come home. I am giving you this bookmark, so you will read the bible and know that God wants you to come back home. That's my wish, I hope you like your bookmark, here are some Starburst candy, maybe they will make you realize you need to come back home, please do."

God wants us to come home to Him, to accept His Son and study His word. You may feel compelled to stop right now and make the greatest decision of your life. It is so simple to receive the greatest gift you will ever have offered to you. All you have to do is ask.

If you want that personal relationship with Jesus Christ and desire peace, happiness and eternal life, read the passages of scripture below. Call out from your heart He will hear your prayer. Please read carefully the plan of salvation and remember. . . . .**All you have to do is ask.**

THE PLAN OF SALVATION

A. Admit you have sinned.
For all have sinned, and come short of the glory of God. Romans 3:23

B. Believe that Jesus died for you sins.
For God so loved the world, that he gave his only begotten Son, that whosoever believeth in him should not perish, but have everlasting life. John 3:16

C. Confess and leave your sins behind.
If we confess our sins, he is faithful and just to forgive us our sins, and to cleanse us from all unrighteousness. 1 John 1:9
There is no perfect righteous person.
"There is no one righteous, not even one;" - Romans 3:10

We all have sinned.
"For all have sinned and fall short of the glory of God."
- Romans 3:23

God loves us, even though we are sinners.
"But God demonstrates His Love for us, in this: while we were still sinners, Christ died for us." - Romans 5:8

The provision - God's Gift.
"For the wages of sin is death, but the gift of God is eternal life in Christ Jesus our Lord." - Romans 6:23

"For it is by the grace you have been saved, through faith - and this not from yourselves, it is the gift of God - not by works, so that no one can boast." - Ephesians 2:8–9

There must be repentance of sin (turning away from sin).
"Repent and believe the Good News!" - Mark 1:15

If you have been questioning God's Love and do not know Him as your Heavenly Father, you can today by accepting His Son Jesus Christ

The required action - believe and confess.
"That if you confess with your mouth that Jesus is Lord,' and believe in your heart that God raised him from the dead, YOU WILL BE SAVED. For it is with your heart that you believe and are justified, and it is with your mouth that you confess and are saved." Romans 10:9–10

THE PRAYER OF SALVATION

Dear Heavenly Father I come to you in the name of your Son Jesus. Lord, I confess that I am a sinner. Lord Jesus, I believe that you are the son of God and that you did died on the cross for me and the forgiveness of my sins.

Right now, Jesus, I place my total trust in you. Lord, come into my heart; forgive me of my sins, and save me. From this day forward, I will live for you. Thank you for saving me. In your Holy name I pray, Amen

If you prayed that pray and accepted Jesus Christ as your Savior, I want to welcome you to the family of God. I trust that you will begin reading your Bible and study God's precious word as you begin your new journey on the real Road to Recovery and happiness through Jesus Christ. Find a good bible believing church and begin experiencing the goodness of God today.

Thank you for taking time to read Building a Blended Family. I trust you will take what you read, apply it to your life, and spread the word to members of your blended family, or someone you know.

May God richly bless and keep you.
In Christ,
Phil Collins

REFERENCES

The New King James Version, (Nashville, TN: Thomas Nelson Publishers) 1998, c1982.

Quick, Donna S. and Botkin, Darla R., "Helping Children in Stepfamilies: Suggestions for Teachers and Child Care Professionals," Kaleidoscope, III, 13–17, 1987.

Turnbull, Sharon K. and Turnbull, James M., "To Dream the Impossible Dream: An Agenda for Discussion with Stepfamilies." Family Relations, 227–229, April 1983.

Holy Bible, New Living Translation, (Wheaton, IL: Tyndale House Publishers, Inc.) 1996.

For information on conference speaking engagements,
seminar presentations, or Building the Blended Family,
contact Phil Collins at
pastorphil1956@yahoo.com,
or visit www.buildingablendedfamily.org

To order more copies of this book:
TATE PUBLISHING, LLC

127 East Trade Center Terrace
Mustang, OK 73064

(888) 361 - 9473

Tate Publishing, LLC

www.tatepublishing.com